知乎 × Wavemaker

关于未来的提问

OUR QUESTIONS TO THE FUTURE

赵林娜 主编

图书在版编目(CIP)数据

关于未来的提问 / 赵林娜主编 .— 上海 : 上海社会科学院出版社，2022
ISBN 978 - 7 - 5520 - 3816 - 3

Ⅰ. ①关… Ⅱ. ①赵… Ⅲ. ①未来学—通俗读物 Ⅳ. ①G303-49

中国版本图书馆CIP数据核字（2022）第107022号

关于未来的提问

主　　编：赵林娜
责任编辑：霍　覃
校　　译：秦心雨
整体设计：周清华
出版发行：上海社会科学院出版社
上海顺昌路622号　邮编200025
电话总机021−63315947　销售热线021−53063735
http: //www.sassp.cn　E-mail: sassp@sassp. cn
排　　版：南京展望文化发展有限公司
印　　刷：上海景条印刷有限公司
开　　本：890毫米×1240毫米　1/32
印　　张：10.875
字　　数：286千
版　　次：2022年9月第1版　　2022年9月第1次印刷

ISBN 978-7-5520-3816-3 / G · 1186　　定价：68.00元

关于未来的提问

Our Questions to the Future

知乎 × Wavemaker

团队介绍

赵林娜（Linna Zhao）
项目发起人，书籍主编
蔚迈品牌咨询与趋势研究负责人

Linna在WPP群邑旗下的新型传播机构 Wavemaker 蔚迈负责趋势研究与咨询（Thought Leadership）。

她关注社会话题与创新，持续出品白皮书与知识分享内容，例如发布历时5年的《中国老龄化社会的潜藏价值》系列报告、《数字时代的中国孩童》、《掀风破浪：中国电商发展新动能》、《中国品质生活白皮书》、《中国健康新态势》、《中国Z世代》、《中国高净值人群情谊往来白皮书》、《时尚中国研究报告》等。

张炎（Robbie Zhang）
联合发起人
知乎商业策略与招商业务负责人

张炎现任知乎商业策略与招商业务负责人，负责知乎公司商业化价值挖掘、品牌打造，以及面向商业化收入的营销解决方案、招商&IP项目等。

2020年，发起“知乎社会创新实验室”，推动知乎在创新公益、社会创新领域的探索。

崔绮雯（Qiwen Cui）
联合发起人
社会创新机构 BottleDream 内容官

崔绮雯是社会创新机构 BottleDream 的内容官，关注气候变化、科技向善等长期公共议题并从事内容创作。2020 年疫情至今，她和 BottleDream 的团队多次参与疫情社会救助和物资调配行动。在此之前，她曾是《好奇心日报》硅谷和北京两地科技记者，关注前沿技术发展及其社会影响。

前言

我们也许认为自己是关心未来的。

为什么不呢？我们可能都在人生大事上认真地思考过未来，比如，是否应该辞职或跳槽，在哪个城市定居，要不要结婚或生育，甚至是生命终点的议题，等等。关心未来好像应该是一件“理所应当”的事。无论思考与否，未来也都将如约而至，我们也终将继续前行。

但是，与其原地等待让未来悄然发生，被动地接受未来的到来，为什么不获得更多的主动权，来更无畏和有掌控感地步入未来呢?

而谈及对未来的思考，就涉及“未来观”的问题，但是“未来观”似乎是缺席的。人们可能会很清晰地说出自己的育儿观、择偶观、择业观……但是，说到“未来观”，你的未来观是怎样的呢?

我们对未来的观感好像天然有着一层灰度的滤镜。回顾影视作品，关于未来的题材多是外星生物入侵、病毒、极端理想、超能人类，以及机器人取代人类之类的主题。比如，《黑客帝国》《异形》《流浪地球》等，关于未来的影视作品似乎在一定程度上达成了“共识”，就是以悲观主义的色调为始，最终秉持正面积极的价值观画上希望的句点。

如果拉近镜头去看尊崇勤奋而务实的中国文化，我想到关于未来观的4个词是：远虑（我们奉行居安思危、未雨绸缪、先天下之忧而忧）、久长（我们的时间线也拉得很长，比如“下辈子”“500年后”“百岁、千岁、万岁”）、非吾（对未来的掌控力好像建立在外在，比如运势、风水、命运）、愿能（我们相信主观能动性，比如人定胜天、长风破浪会有时）。我们的文化更聚焦宏观的视角。

为了获得更多的发现，在2021年的创客运动盛会 Maker Faire（制汇嘉年华）上，我们（蔚迈中国）与知乎一起，在上海外滩发起了一场集体行为艺术。我们收集了来自不同年龄段的好奇宝宝们对未来的提问与想象，用中国的书法艺术与这些提问者共创了一条百米长的提问大道，并邀请现场的参与者通过图像投射共创了一个关于未来的拼贴作品展。

在孩童与成人身上，我们看到了非常明确的分割线。

一方面，在谈论未来时，孩童偏好用“我”这个第一人称的主语；而成人偏好用“人类”“社会”“人们”这样的第三人称主语或非人称主语。

另一方面，孩童的思考更乐观，更具有天马行空的想象力；而成人的思考更冷静，也更聚焦这个世界的大问题，比如，“科技的发展会消除人性中的弱点吗？”“世界何时可以更包容”“什么时候理想主义不再是妄想”“家人与朋友间的关系纽带未来是否会变弱？”

活动现场成人与孩童的提问

100米写满成人和孩子“对未来的提问”的路

贴满“对未来的期待”的拼贴作品展

相较而言，

儿童更……	成人更……
想象	矛盾
微观	宏观
具象	抽象
情感	理性
趣味	合理
正义	秩序

除此以外，我们发现了一个有趣的现象，就是不论成人还是孩童，都特别喜欢问“是”与“否”的问题，好像要透过确定性的问题，获得一个简单的答案。比如，“人类的平均寿命会到100岁吗？”“世界是否会变得无国界化？”“未来全球化的进程是前进还是倒退？”“科技会拉大人与人之间、国与国之间的差距吗？”“污染问题在未来可以得到解决吗？”

我们也许真的需要更加有方法地思考未来。

那么，应该如何做呢？

最重要的一步，就是提问。

哈佛大学的儿童心理学家保罗·哈里斯（Paul Harris）研究发现，从2—5岁，每个孩子平均会提出4万个问题；但是，长大后，我们变得不爱提问题了。提问的数量随着年龄的增长而递减。

所以，千万不要以为提问是一个简单的事，也不要认为这是全人类的本能，即便这个能力是与生俱来的，但随着年龄的增长，提问的动力反而逐年减低了。越长大，兼顾的事情和责任越多，人们就越容易寻求简单直接的答案。思考非常消耗脑力，而大脑是个节能体系，是会尽量避免能耗的。

这也就是为什么，我们和知乎共同发起了“关于未来的提问”这个社会创新项目。

因为知乎相信：有问题，就有答案。

我们相信：有好奇，就有行动。

其实，提问也是有方法和框架体系的。

提问最重要的四个句式是 :“什么 WHAT”“怎么 HOW”“为什么 WHY”和“假如 WHAT IF”。这四个看似简单的句式，支撑了所有我们探索与验证的方式。

“什么WHAT ”和“怎么HOW”用来探索和陈述事实，“为什么WHY ”用来剥洋葱式地进行剖析，“假如WHAT IF”用于提出假设，而接下来的探索、验证与规划又会回到“什么WHAT”“怎么HOW”“为什么WHY”这三个句式。

同样的句式可以延伸出非常多样的提问方式，取决于你的命题和目标。如果是商业领域，我们会针对不同的命题和目标定制化地设计具体的框架，涉及不同的方法论、框架、头脑风暴与共建的方式等，需要根据具体的情况进行设计。

这里只是跟大家分享一个简单的逻辑，而具体支撑每一个步骤去深度探索的，就是这4个关键的提问句式。

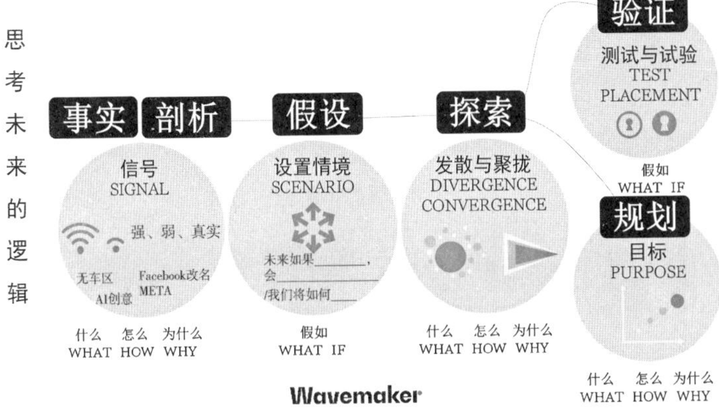

思考未来的基本逻辑图

懂得了提问的重要性和框架，还是不够的，不要忘记设定时间刻度。如果失去了时间刻度，“未来”就变得无比遥远。

可以试着想想看，50年后的未来，你的脑海中会有清晰的画面吗？30年、20年、10年呢？答案应该是不清晰的。但如果是1年呢？是不是有了更多的把握？

让我们把时间刻度打开来看，1年，确实是对未来拥有确定性的临界点。人们更难规划1年以上的事。在新冠肺炎疫情出现之前，境外游这样的长线旅游产品的购买，再低价产品的购买也多集中在1年及以内。对于1年以后会发生的事有更少的把握。

因此，我们需要提升更具确定感的未来，指的是1年以上的，确定性降到可控范围之外的未来。

那么，思考多远的未来会更有意义呢？

答案因人而异。如果要对具体的规划做指引，我们的建议是，以1—2年为近期规划，以3—5年为短期愿景，以10年为期来设置大目标。企业的未来规划也大致是这样的划分。

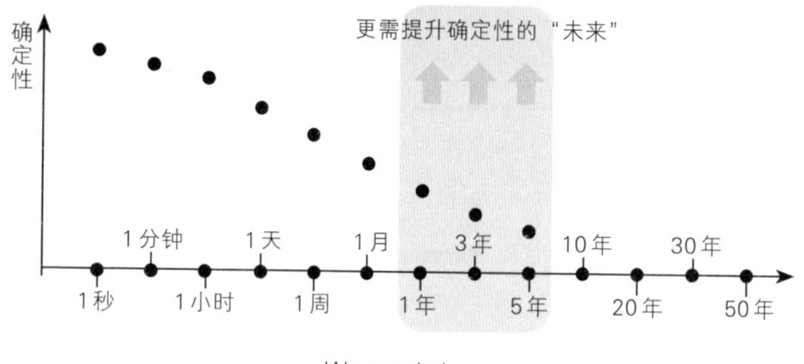

Wavemakei

确定性和时间的对应关系图

这不意味着更远景的未来没有意义（其实一些有前瞻性的企业已经在研究30年和50年后的未来了），只是若要更能指引当下的规划，1—10年为期的时间线更能驱动具体的行动。

在本书中，我们时间的设定是10年。

需要注意的是，这个10年只是一个思考的设定，并不能预测精确事物的发生。比如，谁会想到20世纪50年代就诞生的AI到今天才开始真正发挥作用呢？而智慧城市的发展却因新冠肺炎疫情的出现被超速推动了。

我们在10年的时间设定下，围绕未来跟生活有关的十大图景，展开阐释：

■ 什么WHAT：会发生什么趋势？

■ 怎么HOW：科技如何赋能未来？

■ 为什么WHY：在解决哪些当下的问题？

我们希望能通过这样的内容，启发您思考"假如 WHAT IF"的问题。

因此，您手中的这本书并不是一本方法论的专业书。

我们所希望的，是透过鼓励大家更多地对未来提问，来启发人们更多地思考未来。

当然，提问过后，还有三件同等重要的事。

这三件事是：

一是定义。指的是定义自己的未来价值。

从"我可以做什么"到"我需要做什么"，再到"我必须做什么"，逐层进行筛查，来帮助自己设定人生使命，并转换成具体的目标、计划与行动。

我非常尊敬的袁隆平老先生，就是有非常清晰的个人使命。他做的这件事，是他认为"必须"要做的事，也是他毕生的使命与行动。

世界上价值感最高的品牌，也都懂得如何定义自己未来价值的品牌。比如在BrandZ品牌价值全球排行榜上名列前茅的三个品牌：亚马逊、苹果、微软，他们所设定的行动都是围绕各自的核心使命和信念而展开。

亚马逊相信一切以人为本，他们的价值观里列在第一位的便是联邦最低薪酬，同时尊重LGBTQ的权利。苹果秉持“可用性”为先，让产品为每一个人所用，因此极大力度地推动残疾人等特殊群体的功能应用开发。微软的使命是赋能每一个机构与个人获得更多的成就，因此转换成具体的行动是：创新、AI、可信计算等具体的解决方案。

无论是企业还是个人，都应该在规划前，定义好什么才是自己“必须”去履行的使命。

二是启发。

我们都很难坐在那里凭空想象未来，这个时候就需要用到创意思考工具。

在思考和创意产生的过程中，我们常常在一起头脑风暴，并用特别的工具来刺激想象力，帮助我们投射和表达。有很多种帮助启发的方式，比如：视觉的、听觉的、动觉的、言语的、编剧式、空间、触觉的、嗅觉的，会根据不同的情境进行选择。

我们在Maker Faire的现场仅用了视觉的方式，透过图片拼贴就帮助了很多参与者在10—20分钟内更清晰地思考和表述自己关心的未来。

在这里，我想挑选几幅孩童的作品分享给大家：

一位4岁的孩子告诉我们：未来有机器人陪小朋友去迪士尼，小朋友不会走丢了。

一位5岁的孩子说：希望未来的医院种满鲜花，这样孩子们去了不会害怕。

一位8岁的孩子好奇：如果人类把地球的种子带到别的星球上去种，会长出什么样的植物呢?

一位10岁的孩子希望：未来世界应该为这些经历过痛苦又很努力的人道歉。

一位18岁刚成年的朋友在思考：未来，人类应如何在变化中保留自己的独特性？

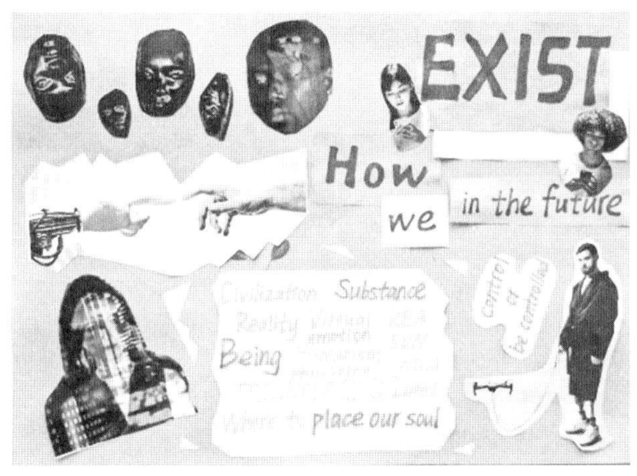

启发我们发掘内心真实的想法，清晰化我们的想象，其实并没有那么难。

当然，除了定义未来价值和启发创造力思维之外，第三件至关重要的事，还是有可行度高的规划与执行力。

定义、启发、执行力这三件事并未在书中聚焦和呈现。

我们更愿先从提问开始，再一步步启发人们产生更多的思考和行动。

最后，愿我们：前路浩荡，勇士一往无前。

赵林娜（Linna Zhao）

写于2021年11月22日

序言

出品方

出品方：蔚迈中国（Wavemaker）

蔚迈是一家集媒介传播、内容营销和科技革新于一身的全球新型代理公司，隶属全球最大的传播集团WPP以及商业媒介投资集团——群邑。

作为一个创新的传播机构，我们以大胆和谨慎的态度去启发、激发进步，并始终对未来的前瞻趋势进行深度剖析。我们分析趋势，并为不同品牌方提供引领时代锐变，聚焦产业洞察与赋有未来庞大商业价值的风向情报前哨站。在通过挑战传统和重塑创意不断引领行业的同时，我们从不忘记关注过去，洞察未来，并在这一过程中，为客户带来独特的视角，展望更好的明天。

我们相信通往未来的道路从来不是单一的。我们与社会科学家、科技企业家等进行了广泛的合作交流，我们逐渐相信，最根本的是“勇气、好奇心和承诺”，提出一个简单的“什么、为什么、如何、如果……该怎么办”的框架清单。这种不引人注意的行为，使世界变得截然不同。很多的“奇迹”隐藏在平淡的映画中，令人惊讶且最重要的是，唯有沉溺于童真般的好奇，提出越来越多能以想象的问题，才能最终把任何可行性相关联的物件变成宜居的用品。

这本书试图将实用性和想象力结合起来，塑造成10个特色小品——每一个小品都勾勒出一个与普通人生活相联共生的未来，不仅激发你去计算，去合理化，而且以一种你可能无法做到或未知的方式与未来联系在一起。

我们希望，在整个旅程中，有此荣幸能邀请你们来加入想象，一同来感受我们的社会结构正在进行技术革新的人性一面，并最终带着更多问题的探索而不是答案，好奇而不是盲然选择放弃或离开。人生的关键往往在于自己的选择，处事思想关乎我们的未来，也会影响着将来能成为什么样的人。

联合出品方：知乎

知乎——有问题，就会有答案。

作为中文互联网高质量的问答社区和创作者聚集的原创内容平台，知乎于2011年1月正式上线，以“让人们更好地分享知识、经验和见解，找到自己的解答”为品牌使命。

知乎可谓是承包了中国网友的脑洞。截至2020年12月31日，知乎累计拥有4 310万名内容创作者，已贡献3.53亿条内容，其中包括3.15亿个问答。知乎每天会新增超过2 000万条创作和互动。知乎多元化内容覆盖1 000多个垂直领域和57.1万个话题。

凭借认真、专业、友善的社区氛围、独特的产品机制以及结构化和易获得的优质内容，知乎聚集了中文互联网科技、商业、影视、时尚、文化等领域最具创造力的人群，已成为综合性、全品类、在诸多领域具有关键影响力的知识分享社区和创作者聚集的原创内容平台，建立起了以社区驱动的内容变现商业模式。

目前，知乎已经覆盖问答社区、会员服务体系“盐选会员”、搜索、热榜等一系列产品和服务，并建立了包括图文、视频、直播等在内的多元媒介形式。

2021年1月13日，知乎将品牌slogan从“有问题，上知乎”更新为“有问题，就会有答案”。

2010年10月15日，知乎的创始人周源，致知乎团队全体的信，记录了最初的想法：我们相信一点，在垃圾泛滥的互联网信息海洋中，真正有价值的信息是绝对的稀缺品，知识——被系统化、组织化的高质量信息——都还存在于个体大脑中，远未得到有效的挖掘和利用。知乎提供了一个产生、分享和传播知识的工具，我们鼓励每个人都来分享知识，将每个人的知识都聚集起来，并为人人所用。

我们为什么写这本书

活在当下！
今朝有酒今朝醉！
及时行乐（Carpe Diem）！
加了感叹号，是用来做强调的。

我们自古重视当下，拼搏奋斗与对生活的享受与珍视仿佛都主要针对的是于当下而言。这在如今同样能收获不同代际的共鸣。

而在西方，近2 000年来，及时行乐（*Carpe Diem*）被隐藏在历史的一个不起眼角落里，一夜之间，罗宾·威廉姆斯在《死亡诗社》中的精彩表演，使他成为众人瞩目的焦点。

把每一天都当作最后一天来过，让明天的烦恼成为明天的烦恼。

的确，为什么不呢？许多人认为，若是放眼第三个千年的到来，将会是更具人类文明智慧及科技跃进的新时代。国际贸易蓬勃发展，以历史上无与伦比的速度开启了越来越多的技术进步，我们的大部分生活将被智能科技带来的便利所覆盖，也同时为每个忙碌者的理想追求腾出了更多的时间与空间。

当生活确实变得更加美好的时候，我们也始终相信着，科学技术正在继续朝着正确的方向快速发展，将来会有更加智慧整合且通合人性的多元生活科技，持续陪伴和改进着我们的精致生活。因此，未来不再是那么遥不可及或充满不切实际的幻想，而是将我们生活中的实际需求，在科学技术的进步上，达到人类的最高生活理想。所以，我们想要试图勾勒出的，是基于生活确定需求和场景的，更为明确和踏实的，关于未来的好奇与想象。

诚然，生活在这世间，有时会出现意想不到的烦恼，这的确让我们十分无奈，想想在接下来的日子里，我们会不会一次又一次地被提醒和面对，反复发生的金融危机、疾病暴发、武装冲突、难民被迫流离失所——当人类面临未知突发灾难时，事件的冷酷无情，又将再次考验着人性使然。比如新冠肺炎疫情让世界不同国家的人们都拥有了共同的记忆，体会到不确定的未来及人生无常的无奈。

虽然未来不是100%可直接预测的，但它并没有阻止我们去想象、去向往、去追求，并祝福着我们手中的未来会更好。

但是，如果科技创造者只为自身商业利益，而罔顾社会人性道德，任由技术自生自灭是非常不明智的。我们需要更多的探索。我们必须扪心自问，不仅是我们如何来到这里的，更重要的是，我们必须做些什么，才能忠于我们内心的方向，在正确的指引下走上一条更好的道路？简言之，我们需要开始向自己提出更多的问题并深度思考，启发着面对更多是与非的自己。

尽管提出问题这件事并不在乎难与不难，因为人类天生就是提问者，但要不断地让自己坚持去提问却并不容易。讽刺的是，社会上似乎也飘荡着一种无所谓的声音，和“与世无争”的躺平心态。诚然，这也是一种生活态度与活法，但似乎少了些对未来无限可能的向往和追求。此外，关于技术进步方面的空前突破——尤其是对于那些生活在城市中的人来说，相当一部分日常已经被分配到智能机器或云端算法上，他们的生活机能已经变得十分方便和舒适。如此一来，我们便更容易陷入现代生活的舒适陷阱，忘了曾经的自己对未来抱有的好奇和初心。

我们必须从理所当然的安逸中清醒过来，让自己重获对未来的好奇与大胆设想的求知欲，让我们在这个世界上可以更真实地活着。期待未来，并不意味着盲目地等待未知发生，而是思考既有现实可以如何蜕变和再创造。同时，我们需要确保我们自己的科技发明，仍然是你我共同创造更美好明天的原动力。换言之，为了生活在一个更加包容、高效和可持续的未来，我们需要检视一直以来的做事方式，重新学习如何变得好奇、富有想象力、大胆、创新，以及最关键的是，“迈出提出问题的第一步”——无论你这件事有多么简单。

我们相信，到目前为止，是什么让我们成了真正的我们，是真正的好奇心和背后的无数问题，激励着我们不断向前，并最终引发思考和要求答案，将我们带到未来梦想要去的地方。

来自编者的感谢

我不是这本书的作者。因为这本书是由很多伙伴们一同用心不计日夜来共创完版。

在撰写这本书的过程中，我们选择了诸多不同的问题，也与不同背景的人交谈，咨询了不同行业的专家——所有的准备、研究与探讨，都是为了让我们的读者变得更加好奇，提出更多的思考与问题。

如果没有我在Wavemaker和其他公司的同事和朋友，以及知乎背后强大的专业团队奉献支持，这一作品也就不会出现在这与各位相见，很开心能与一群五湖四海志同道合、充满热情与希望的伙伴，做了这样非常有意义的作品，能提供给大家一些新的思路，再加些新的观点，让我们可以尽情地想象，去质疑，去探索，去寻找那些看似不容易得到的“答案”。

在Wavemaker团队中，我诚挚地感谢Gordon Domlija、Jose Campon、Ann Lim, Henry Wang、Hadassah Chen、Roy Zhang、Lisa Dai、Lynn Lin、Bin Hu、Louis Zheng、Talise Zhou、Rio Liu、Katy Sun、Chloe Zhao、Yulie Zhu、

Zaida Cai、Kelvin Lau、Patty Shao、Vikas Lin，我十分有幸与他们相识，他们对我产生了很大的正面影响。

特别是，我要对Charlotte Wright表示感谢，感谢她坦率地指出并改善了初版书稿的局限性问题；以及Nic McCarthy 对于这本书选择以更诗意的方式设置基调的支持；也要特别感谢Jeffrey Wang，他帮助我们重新构思了这个故事的英文版本，除了一般的介绍，更多一点韵味，以及王博霖在此书中文含义的提炼上，给予了非常大的帮助。

我特别由衷地感谢来自知乎的伙伴们，他们对完善提问的坚定追求给了我极大的启发。

以及知乎上关心未来的朋友们，感谢他们愿意与我们分享那些对未来十大图景发出大胆的提问。

怀着无比激动的心情，再次感谢所有为这本书的诞生做出贡献的人，当我们分享其中许多问题，也同时引导着我们思考在那些未知的时间边界，等待我们的是什么。我们期待实现的是透过兴趣启发能邀请你们加入我们的思考和提出问题，关于一个尚待绘制的空间时间，一个我们可以一起跋涉走向的共同未来。我们希望我们的问题能引起足够的好奇兴趣，一旦你们开始尽情地质疑“Carpe Diem”[*]的传统智慧，我们的想象便会逐渐明晰地勾勒出来，让你们对无数明天的无限可能充满好奇。

赵林娜（Linna Zhao）
上海，2021年

* Carpe Diem是一句拉丁谚语，意为“及时行乐，活在当下”。

请收下我们写给你的诗歌与信

知乎关于未来的诗歌：

没办法
这样的问题
就是留给我们这代人的
有人举手发问
谁能帮中国拿一个诺贝尔文学奖？
莫言举手，作了回答
有人举手发问
盐碱地里能不能种出水稻？
袁隆平举手，作了回答
很多人举手发问
除了京剧、功夫和中餐
我们还有什么东西可以分享给全世界？
刘慈欣举手，作了回答

全世界举手发问
一个国家最宝贵的财富是什么？
钟南山、张文宏们
举手代表无数中国人作了回答
无数人在举手发问
我们应该如何生活
如何思考如何走出困境
如何应对挑战
如何寻找乐趣
如何探寻真相
因为数不清的崭新的问题
尚未记录在人类出版过的一切书籍上
未曾听闻于前辈口口相传的经验里
不知不觉
我们走到了无人区
已经没人可以教我们
应该怎么做
我们要举手发问
路向何处求？
但世界上每一个问题
终究会找到它的答案
因为答案并不在未知的未来
它藏在每一个人的大脑里
每一个人的生活里

每一个人走过的脚印里

只要举起手来

向着无数的人分享我们的知识、经验和见解

曾经一个人走过的路

就变成了无数人的路

2011年1月，知乎上线后的第一个问题

如何正确使用知乎

到今天

有超过4 400万个问题

问所有你想得到的问题、想不到的问题

有超过2.4亿个回答

用文字、用图片、用视频、用直播

就在一问一答之间

我们一起战胜了，未知带来的恐惧与焦虑、傲慢与偏见

就在一问一答之间

我们变成了路灯

一座路灯只能照亮100米的旅程

没关系

数以亿计的路灯

可以照亮这颗星球上所有的路

但这远远不够

还有太多问题

不问不快

我们要举起手来发问

你要相信

你的问题，也是无数人的问题

我们要举起手来回答

你要相信

你的答案，能给无数人答案

我们相信

在这个世界上

有人提问。就一定有人回答

知乎有问题。就会有答案

这代人的问题

会找到这代人的答案

一封 Wavemaker 的来信

高顿（Gordon Domlija）
CEO，蔚迈亚太地区

坚决履行我的个人座右铭：“永远朝着更好的方向”。

1.0 – 未来已至，思考先行

我们似乎怀着复杂的心情送走了2020。

无论你的体会感觉是如何，在这一年，该发生的（新常态）加速发生了，不该发生的（新冠肺炎疫情）也无法避免。

2020年注定是我们人类历史上永载史册难以忘却的一年。

一场猝不及防的疫情，打乱了我们以往日常的生活。这一场“黑天鹅事件”使不同国家与不同民族，产生了共同的深刻记忆，有人彷徨不安，有人泰然自若，也有人重振旗鼓负重前行。

面对未来的不确定性和正在催生的新事物，每个个体和企业都需要凭借自己最珍贵的生命韧性去应变及坦然面对。无论是企业和个人，都加快了转念、转变和转型的步伐，重新审视当下、思考未来。

而与此同时，这一年也因一些新兴概念而记入史册，5G元年、万物互联、边缘计算、金融科技、禁塑脱碳等，也足以让这个年代不负“未来”之名。

2020，这个在10年前看来还有着未来感的年份，却并不像科幻小说里描写的那般奇妙与虚幻。科幻作品里的“未来”总是超前于实际的，每每到来时，你总会发现理想和现实不对称的鸿沟与差距。

这往往体现出的，是人们对“未来”的想象认知，作为一个不太具体又模糊的存在，它好像总是离我们很遥远，也似乎应该离我们很远。也因此，很多人错过了对未来的深度思考和探寻筹谋。

然而，“未来”总是悄然而至，无论你是否秣马厉兵。

未来已至，思考的人早已整装出发。

何塞（Jose Campon）
CEO, 蔚迈中国

相信被好奇心所驱使的激情，会让我们的生活更加有趣。

2.0 – 期待美好的意外

没有人有透视未来的水晶球。如果说过去的几十年教会了我们一些东西的话，那就是有一些即将改变我们生活的事件在等着我们，没有人能够精准预测，甚至无法触碰边际想象。

在西班牙，有一种说法是“我们对未来唯一的了解就是100年后，我们都会离去”。阐述着对未来的预测几乎没有把握，试图预测未来也不是绝对科学。

让我们从一个粗糙的现实开始：作为人类，我们可以预期会有的利益损失、社会问题、某种生存危机和生活担忧，比如社会和国家政策之间的分歧日益扩大……而我们不能没有危机意识或完全认为没有什么大问题，但这确实也是生活的一部分，难道不是吗？无论我们究竟经历了什么，作为人类，我们都有一套相似的在心中的感受和感觉……这是人类大脑中自然的化学反应。

当今，中国显然站在乐观的一面，似乎没有什么可以输掉的，而一切都可以战胜的。非常积极的精神氛围鼓励着人们大气果敢地去干实事，去积极努力克服着所有问题，着手未来，勇者无惧。中国还有着一种在西方看不到的技术天赋。这股新兴的创造力正开始树立标杆。例如，亚马逊从阿里巴巴的书中摘取了一页，搭建了广告业务。我也非常密切地关注着Shein——一家中国公司在快速时尚行业完全颠覆了供应链，实时进行设计和生产。

因此，我相信未来是开放、独特又融合的。它与所有的可能性相关，并能打破你围绕自己建立的过去的限制。

同时，我也想分享我个人的真实体会。在我的人生经历中，我改变了很多次我的生活和身份，甚至有时我自己都难以想象我会做出这样的改变。

所以，你真的可以重新想象和重塑你自己、你自己的身份，为什么不呢？有时候只是问一个简单的问题，然后二话不说地去挑战。

做一个敢于冒险的斗士，不要只选择活在空有的期盼和等待中，我相信，生命中美好的意外一定会给我们带来最好的时光。

王晟宇（Henry Wang）
首席产品官，蔚迈中国

热衷于在远见和行动之间寻求平衡。

3.0 – 让好奇心推动进步

如果把时间拉回至100年前，会有多少人相信“互联网”会影响改变了世界？而如果是50年前，有多少人会相信一台机器能在10年内击败一位世界大师级棋手？又会有多少人能想象4年前，像抖音这样的中国社交应用能赢得全世界年轻人的青睐喜爱？

纵观历史，这个世界上产生了无数的文明碎片，拼凑出使我们走上了今天的道路。尤其是由于最近信息与技术行业的飞速发展（以及他们的销售人员！），让我们所生活的环境空间，看起来像是一个科幻世界。但回归现实层面，我们能说真的是这样的吗？各位，请别误会我的意思。今天的世界充满了许多奇迹，但是即便像天气预报这样“简单”的事情，我们还是不能准确进行，甚至是超过2周的预测，到目前也还没能实现。而2020年出现的“黑天鹅事件”，没有任何人能够在新冠肺炎疫情发生之前做出预测。

但这并不是说科幻世界是不切实际、只凭空想象的，这只是我们人类伟大旅程的一个组成部分。如果我们定义“科幻小说的终极世界”是进程的100%，不要假设我们已经站在了90%的节点上，每个人就会朝向100%自动前进。我们最有可能发展的极限也只有50%，剩下的创新将是人与机器的组合。即在机器继续提升效率的同时，让人类得以持续性地进行勇敢的新探索。

因此，好奇心也一如既往重要。正是因为未来能进一步提升效率，我们才可以更快地测试新想法，并实践推动具有规模性的时代影响力。关于未来的进步，终将归结为不断突破无限可能的、富有想象力的最强大脑。

蔚迈的其他小伙伴也想对打开书的你提问

关于生活与工作

Vikas：科技为我们“省下来”的时间会被其他什么事物“绑架”和消耗？

Zaida：未来的家务还需要人去做吗？

Patty：我们未来大部分时间会在哪里办公？
同事之间将以什么样的形式协同合作？

Kelvin：科技是为我们赋能还是会替代我们？

Tony：未来科技会使人的价值被挤压吗？

Linna：未来每个人是否都会为自己的热爱而奋斗？

关于和平、爱与关系

Rose：未来会出现解决大小纷争更好的方式吗？

Linna：未来的人们是否会对这个世界和生灵抱有更大的善意？

Katy：未来家人与朋友间的关系纽带是否会变弱？

Linna：未来我们将如何维系核心的关系和各种不同的关系网？

关于人口、地球与宇宙

Chloe：老龄化、少子化的趋势会让地球人口剧减吗？

Arts：人类的平均寿命会到100岁吗？
未来的老年生活是什么样的？

Kelvin：世界是否会变得无国界化？

Emily & Chloe：未来全球化过程是前进还是倒退？

Yulie：科技会拉大人与人之间、国家与国家之间的差距吗？

Zaida：科技会造成贫富差距吗？“赛博朋克”的时代是否会到来？

Arts：未来污染问题会解决吗？植被会越来越少吗？
冰山会彻底融化吗？珍稀物种会灭绝吗？

Emily：未来地球资源会不会枯竭？

Chloe：未来我们会不会遇见外星人？

Rose：未来我们是否会在宇宙中找到第二个家园？

关于消费与出行

Zaida： 未来线下商店还会存在吗？
他们的角色会发生什么样的转变？

Zaida： 当货币完全数字化后，会对现有的线上支付世界产生怎样的影响？

Patty： 自动驾驶普及之后，道路交通是否会变得更加有效率？

Tony： 未来会不会有为电动车充电的马路？

目录

一、开篇：塑造未知

进步似乎总是伴随着意外。时钟嘀嗒作响，环境生态失衡——大气层加速变薄、野火肆虐、冰河溶解等种种问题，在我们这个时代，已经呈现出空前未有的生存紧迫感。那么，我们要去哪里？

让我们从以下4个问题，开始对未来的思考吧！

1. 作为人类意味着什么？

人体机能蜕变增强 ---------- 009

2. 我们之间的关系越来越紧密了吗？

模棱两可之间：超级连接的承诺与模糊 ---------- 010

3. 我们的需求将是数据总和吗？

网络安全和数据所有权 ---------- 012

4. 科技将把我们带向何方？又是谁引领着技术发展？

技术民主化 ---------- 013

二、关于未来的十大生活图景

基于确切的技术和人文趋势，我们用生动易懂的场景勾勒出未来生活的样子。同时，分享我们关于未来的乐观预想与疑问，提出关于未来的关键问题，以及商业灵感和营销机遇。

1. 未来的旅行　019—027

知乎上网友的脑洞提问：

人类如果要星际旅行，目前哪些问题还没有解决？应该怎么样解决？乘上哆啦A梦里的时光机，你想穿梭去哪个时代？

我们对未来的关切提问：

旅行的终极意义是什么？而其边界仅在于时间、空间与文化吗？

未来旅行的关键词：

时光机旅行　除了克服语言和文化障碍，尽情探索未知而不受限制，还要身入其中穿越古今！

虚拟虫洞　在时间和空间之间航行

2. 未来的成长（1）——人才　028—036

知乎上网友的脑洞提问：

未来和算法、机器进一步融合后，人类的智力会有怎样的跃升？当每个人都可以无所不能，人类会进一步追求什么？

我们对未来的关切提问：

未来的我们是否会实现更多的人生价值？那时的我们是否是快乐的？

未来人才的关键词：

超π型人才 睿智通才+多领域专家

2. 未来的成长（2）——学习 037—044

知乎上网友的脑洞提问：

如果可以在1天内学会一件很难的事，你最想学什么？20年后，实体学校会消失吗？

我们对未来的关切提问：

未来的学习如何在由下而上的自我需求与由上至下的“必学内容”间获得平衡？必学内容，如文化传承、道德文明等知识。

未来学习的关键词：

人性化体验式学习 适合个体需求与学习方式的体验式学习

3. 未来的工作 045—053

知乎上网友的脑洞提问：

人工智能替代大部分工作后，还能剩下什么工作给人类呢？
在工作和生活边界越来越模糊的未来，我们如何好好生活？

我们对未来的关切提问：

在未来，工作的形态与方式将会有着如何颠覆性的改变？怎样的工作形态才是工作与生活平衡的最佳形态？

未来工作的关键词：

“随心所欲，自由切换”——工作生活一体化

工作伴随着生活，而生活则伴随着工作！

数字游侠儿：跨时空的自由工作者

自由选择工作空间，规避传统的空间限制

4. 未来的娱乐 054—062

知乎上网友的脑洞提问：

当“虚拟”成为“现实”，我们如何更好地游走在两个世界？
两个能预知未来并且都想赢的人，玩剪刀、石头、布，谁会赢？

我们对未来的关切提问：

在未来，娱乐还会是“娱乐”吗？而我们将仍是参与者还是获得娱乐体验的主导权？

未来娱乐的关键词：

浸入与否 随时随地畅快连接、浸入感官式的体验

情感沉浸 不做旁观者！成为参与者与主角，创造属于我的娱乐体验

5. 未来的消费 063—071

知乎上网友的脑洞提问:

实体门店还有未来吗?可持续产品,是未来的新消费主义吗?

我们对未来的关切提问:

未来,我们如何平衡理性与感性,做出最具价值的消费判断?

未来消费的关键词:

一千个人,一千个哈姆雷特　个人化、定制化、更高效的购物体验

玩乐买买买　体验式零售,启发式选择

6. 未来的家庭 072—081

知乎上网友的脑洞提问:

在未来,住宅的发展趋势和设计思路可能会是怎样的?未来30年或更长久的可预见未来,中国家庭结构模式会有怎样的变化?

我们对未来的关切提问:

未来,何以为家?

未来家庭的关键词:

家+　集多元功能于一身的家

智能家属　无微不至的智能管家

7. 未来的社区 082—091

知乎上网友的脑洞提问：

未来10年，我们的社区生活会因科技发生怎样的变化？ 未来，共享“共居”会是一种主流形态吗？

我们对未来的关切提问：

未来的社区是否会帮助实现生活本应拥有的样子?

未来社区的关键词：

社区生态化 多功能化和社会生态可持续的中心社区

8. 未来的健康 092—101

知乎上网友的脑洞提问：

未来医学可以根治近视吗？ 现代人都变得有头部前倾的倾向了吗？应如何预防？

我们对未来的关切提问：

在未来，我们能否更轻松管理自己以及家人在不同人生阶段的健康状况？

未来健康的关键词：

智能健康管理伴一生

全面设计的医疗保健行业，涵盖所有生命阶段

9. 未来的社交 102—111

知乎上网友的脑洞提问：

社恐症在虚拟社交中，可以被治愈吗？ 如果你可以选择拥有虚拟国籍，你幻想加入怎样的虚拟国度？

我们对未来的关切提问：

在未来，更复杂的社交关系和多元身份会如何拓宽我们生命的宽度？

未来社交的关键词：

平行世界中的多重自我 不同空间的不同身份

10. 未来的数据资产 112—121

知乎上网友的脑洞提问：

数据能怎样更好地帮我们回顾过去？或启发未来的路？把一个人大脑里所有数据都存储上传，能让人脱离肉体永生吗？

我们对未来的关切提问：

我们的数据将成为带来价值的资产，还是冗余的负累？

未来数据资产的关键词：

数据资产化 个人数据成为所有权受法律保护的资产

结 语 123

一

开篇：塑造未知

我们从哪里来？我们是什么？我们要去哪里？

有时，是否自我内心也会思考着，关于人类生命存在意义，思考着所谓的“人生”究竟何为？

“我们从哪里来？我们是什么？我们要去哪里？”像这样看似无声的自我对话，往往是我们与内心触碰的感知，能产生有声的交流。

在中国，我们的文化非常重视“根源”，已经非常习惯且自然地关注“从哪来”的问题。我们讲求传承、祭拜先祖，我们非常自豪地背诵上下五千年的历史与文化内容。这是令我非常骄傲的事。但是，说到“到哪去”的问题，仿佛进入了一个相较之下略为虚空的话题。中国文化讲究中庸之道和博爱精神，讲究勤勉团结与实干精神，而关乎未来的看法似乎更像是一种对人生的态度。

“山重水复疑无路，柳暗花明又一村。”

“长风破浪会有时，直挂云帆济沧海。”

“天命不足畏。”

“鹰击长空，鱼翔浅底，万类霜天竞自由！”

过去与当下好像总是比未来获得了相对更多的关注。

在西方，19世纪，当查尔斯·达尔文发表进化论后不久，法国画家保罗·高更（Paul Gauguin），摆脱了当时传统印象派的作画束缚，将最直观的艺术灵感，用最真实的色彩毫不保留地抒发在作品上，赋予了观众们独立思考领悟的意义价值，其代表作之一便是《我们从何处来？我们是谁？我们向何处去？》的巨作。当人们对自然选择理论的看法一方面是完全的敌视，另一方面是不以为然的怀疑时，高更的绘画作品提出了一种对于存在主义的强烈疑问。

100多年后，在经历了两次人类灾难性的世界大战、无数局部规模的武装冲突、气候产生的干旱、贫困带来的饥荒、病毒突变的死亡疾病相继暴发之后，21世纪的人们，对“我们从何而来？我们又是什么？”也许各自已有了一些认知吧。但还有最后那个老问题:“接下来的我们想要去哪里？”换句话说，就是什么样的未来在等着我们？从《星际迷航》的战后无限乐观，到《银翼杀手》的老套反乌托邦技术，未来在不同的时代总是意味着不同的东西——或多或少存在的希望与绝望，无形拉扯着来回之间的无定性。然而，随着科技的日新月异，带给我们更加智能、便利且不断进化的生活，但也将人们的一切变得越来越固化。当数字技术带来前所未有的进步速度，似乎让我们当中的许多人，陷入了一种自鸣得意的麻木状态，比如：只想去探索下一代iPhone或Netflix的类似热门商品，忽略了社交媒体缩短了我们的注意力广度。眼睛盯着屏幕，屏幕上总是等待着下一次刷新。我们对科技的内在价值所带来更加美好未来的信念，已经类似一种宗教信仰。历史学家兼作家罗纳德·赖特评论说，令人担忧的是，正如市场激进主义在毫无预警的情况下催生了毁灭性的危机，破坏了人们的生计一样，这种普遍认为技术将解决自己制造的所有问题的信念，已经变得与宗教信仰非常类似，导致过去已经有一些社会问题崩溃和人性道德的危机爆发。赖特警告说，未来并不总是更好。进步并不总是带来意料之中的结果。时钟嘀嗒作响，环境生态失衡——大气层加速变薄、野火肆虐、冰河溶解等种种问题，在我们这个时代，已经呈现出空前未有的生存紧迫感。

那么我们要去哪里？
未来是什么？
未来又会是什么？

无论是通过宗教、洞穴绘画或不朽的雕塑，人类总是以某种奇异而难以言喻的方式，与过去或未来的时间共存。

英语中future一词来源于拉丁语futurus，是esse的future分词，在字面意义上指：是，或将是。而我们的中华文明，在看待事物时，无论是现在还是其他方面，总有着与此不同的中庸态度。

未来的现在中文词——未来（wèilái）——字面意思与西方较为一致，意思是尚未到来的事物。而骨子里，我们要“实干”得多。中国古代对未来的表达多是比较近的日期，比如将来（现在之后）、明朝（明天早晨）、明日（明天）、来日（未来某日）等。这是一种非常实际而有趣的文化共识和心态。我们似乎更在意可承诺或规划的近景。而稍微远一些的充满变革的“未来”在意识里似乎有些缺席。“现在能抓什么”永远比“未来需要什么”获得更多的关注。

但是，无论如何，尽管不同文明之间在语言和其他方面存在差异，但归根结底，对地球上的人类来说，“未来”并不是一个非解不可的难题。斗转星移，我们在时间的维度上一步步前行，无数的当下，也在瞬间被转录成了记忆，或被遗弃。无论安定或惶恐，迈进未来也将是我们唯一的出路。尤瓦尔·赫拉利在《人类简史》一书中写到，在有记载的历史的大部分时间里，人类面临的三个主要问题：战争、饥饿、疾病，似乎在世界的某些地区几乎消失了，在其他地区也正在消失，我们有可能面临另一个历史的终结时刻。

那么，你还想要去了解未来吗?

是生存还是毁灭，这是个深思未知的问题。但至于问还是不问，至少对孩子们来说，毕竟不是什么多难的抉择。

沃伦·伯格在*A more beautiful question*中引用了保罗·哈里斯的研究发现：孩子们在这个陌生的星球上生活到5岁之前，平均要问4万个问题。正是通过将强烈的好奇心转化为具体的问题这一过程，我们才能在学习为人的过程中，将意义赋予人和物。比如，第一次看到镜中的自己，试图去理解这个陌生世界中的无数个昨天、今天和明天。但是，随着日复一日，朝起夕落，昼夜更替，那些过去的质疑和想象，曾经天马行空的创造，也逐渐逝去。

当孩子长大成人，“提问”却变成了直接接受的“答案”。

但幸运的是，世界总不乏充满好奇心的人在推动历史进步的车轮。

纵观古今，正是这种提出琐碎而深度问题的能力——无论是否有严格的论究必要性——都为我们带来了突破与思辨。正是我们每个人身上都有着的那颗好奇的初心，在面对难以克服的艰难时刻，给了我们希望与方向。

知乎自10年前成立以来，已收获了4 400多万个问题，这些问题是由中国社会各界人士提出的，涉及的话题广泛，从微观到宇宙无所不包。他们每个人都在提问，邀请，让我们产生探询本质的好奇，使我们在思考中多走一步，并同时互相提出更为详尽和细分解的思考和解答。像它的数百万用户一样，知乎相信，若要勇敢无惧地步入未来，没有什么比更勇敢地提问更好的办法了。有问题，才会有答案。

在Wavemaker，我们总是向员工、客户和合作伙伴提出有关未来的尖锐问题，因为，不仅要活在明天，还要预见和理解今天。我们是坚定的营销与品牌传播实践者，我们相信:“好奇心，是人类进步的驱动力”，我们共同探索一个我们期待的未来。在这个时代，人类和技术已经空前紧密地连接和合作在一起。我们目睹了不可逆转的时代趋势，尽管它们彼此之间似乎还存在着严重的自相矛盾和与情境脱钩的问题。

托马斯·莫尔时代以来的乌托邦梦想是否有一天能实现？《黑客帝国》所展现的场景会不会成为现实？

不是所有问题都会有明确的答案。但每一个答案一定来自好奇心驱使的提问。

现在，我们将透过与生存息息相关的各种提问来探索未来。通过简单的提问行为，我们可以先迈出一步，去憧憬、理解和感受未来。

如果足够幸运、准备足够充分，我们甚至可以早一步迈入想象中的未来。

1. 作为人类意味着什么？

人体机能蜕变增强

是什么定义了我们能力的边界？先天的还是后天的？这一直是周而复始地困扰着很多人的问题。

不同的文化里，都有对人类身体极限与超能力的幻想。

未来的人类能获得像孙悟空或“雷神”* 般的强健的躯体和“火神”** 般的顽强的精神力吗？人们之间的语言隔阂会不会因为点击一个按钮而消失？我们的后代会不会被赋予翅膀、夜视、鳃，就像希腊神话里厄庇墨透斯（Epimetheus）在造人时忘了赐给人类的一样？

在古希腊人的露天剧场中上演的一幕幕戏剧讲述的往往是——人类就是反复无常的诸神的玩物，即使在战胜了敌人，取得最辉煌的胜利之后，也会遭到残酷命运的捉弄。

在菲利普·K.迪克（Philip K. Dick）的《仿生人会梦见电子羊吗？》（*Do Androids Dream of Electric Sheep?*）——而后被雷德利·斯科特（Ridley Scott）改编为电影《银翼杀手》（*Blade Runner*）而为人们所熟知——影片中描绘了这样的场景：在未

* 雷神（Thor），即雷神托尔，是美国漫威漫画旗下的超级英雄。

** 火神（Vulcan），美国漫威漫画中的强大的变种人，拥有操纵庞大能量的能力，能抵抗精神控制。

来的加州没有阳光的天空下，人类在零摩擦的合成环境中生存，安装了机械植入物，和与真人难分真假的完美机器人一起生活。

在进入21世纪的头20年里，人体的机能虽然没有显著的进步。但是，增强人类的本体原始功能或者说利用人体科学技术来强化人类现有的身体（生理和心理）构造潜力的超能力，这些问题再一次被推向了社会关注的前沿。无论是增强注意力控制的“化学兴奋剂”，帮助残疾人士再次行走的“外骨骼套装”，还是将我们重新定位到全新全息世界的VR护目镜，人类增强（Human augmentation）将在许多方面获得进步，并会在本世纪内就重新定义“人类”的概念。

先撇开机械共生不谈，想想如果当技术普及后，早已沉溺于互联网的我们将会如何被改造呢？

2. 我们之间的关系越来越紧密了吗？

模棱两可之间：超级连接的承诺与模糊

社会学家费孝通先生曾用“差序格局”来描述中国人亲疏远近的人际格局，如同水面上泛开的涟漪，延伸开去，一圈一圈，按距离自己的远近来划分亲疏。因而，对于我们而言，重要的还是更亲近的关系。

如今，在智能设备的包围下，有时会令人思考，人与人之间的联系与关系究竟应该是怎样的。对于有些人来说，只需点击几下鼠标或手机就可以认识陌生人，但这并不能告诉我们，我们如何与更为重要的人建立实质的关系，去相互理解和感受。

是否像华金·菲尼克斯在斯派克·琼斯2013年的电影《她》（*Her*）中绝望地爱上了智能操作系统（OS）那样建立关系的一种新的方式？还是仅仅反映了未来的人们会越来越无力与不同于自己的其他人打交道？

今天的新生儿将来可能将会以我们完全无法想象的方式生活，但若缺少了父母正确健康的引导，也许未来将出现更多的孤独成瘾者。许多过去的常识放到现在显然已经过时了，更不要说去适用于未来。不管怎样，我们将不得不在未来的许多日子里独自起程。也许以后隔着屏幕去端详挚亲好友的照片真的能带给我们真实的思念与感受，也许我们会慢慢习惯于更多缺少物理连接的关系。

也许会，也许不会。

那么，未来，超级连接下将会被增强的真实感受，是否会让人们陷入这模糊的陷阱？

3. 我们的需求将是数据总和吗?

网络安全和数据所有权

这是一段颠覆时代的无畏宣言:"工业世界的政府，你们这些肉体和钢铁的巨人，令人厌倦，我来自赛柏空间，思维的新家园。以未来的名义，我要求属于过去的你们，不要干涉我们……我们将在赛柏空间创造一种思维的文明，这种文明将比你们这些政府此前所创造的更为人道和公平。"[1]1996年，在瑞士达沃斯，约翰·巴娄和其他互联网爱好者，以不屈不挠的热情和乐观的态度，宣布了新商业化全球互联网络的独立与人权平等共融性。当时的他们或我们中的许多人，几乎不知道接下来到底会发生什么?!

今天，操作日趋简便，不用动脑便可以尽情无限畅游任一网络平台，但我们是否忽略了曾经在网上留下的痕迹?个人的隐私数据该如何保护，不该四处传播?谁有权访问我们生成的数据，以及他们是如何使用这些数据的?随着科技巨头们忙于利用数据所有权的模糊性，学者们也忙于争论建立合法数据权利意味着什么。在20世纪第10个年头，国际社会秩序上接二连三地曝出丑闻——个人隐私泄密和黑客攻击越来越多。随着资讯平台泛滥，网络上出现了违法应用隐私数据的行为，而与此同时越来越多的人也意识到缺乏数字财产防护所带来的

1《赛博空间独立宣言》，1992年2月8日。

风险。

无论是好是坏，在跨越国度不分种族、日益互联的世界中，我们的数字生活及其足迹比我们在工作和休闲中的实际存在发挥着更为重要的作用，在这一点上似乎是难以避免的。我们将不得不接受这样一个事实：无论我们多抱有希望，或毫无寄望，网络空间肯定不会成为一个纯洁的世外桃源。恰恰相反，网络将一如既往地成为一个高度动态、包容、时常发生混乱的地方，就像屏幕前的各种可能的地方一样。因此，我们是否愿意尽一切努力，使之成为一个更公平、更理智、更人道至上的地方呢?

4. 科技将把我们带向何方？又是谁引领着技术发展？

技术民主化

美国哲学家安德鲁·芬伯格（Andrew Feenberg）在其2002年首次出版的名著《技术批判理论》（*Transforming Technology*）中提醒我们，应当让把握技术霸权的精英承担起整个社会阶层的责任，同时让整体公众参与技术设计，最终实现一种技术协同，而不是让某一阶层独霸技术的设计权而导致失衡，并给世界其他地区带来可怕的后果。他认为，未来技术的发展方向应该是开放的，所有人都可以参与和获取，从而在技术与环境完全协同的意义上实现真正的进步。

在许多方面，这预示着开源、开放存取和许多类似的事成为主流。随着政策制定者意识到要更多地强调利益相关者而不仅仅是股东的呼声，技术民主化的趋势，正在迅速改变我们日常生活中的社会形态，从金融（如加密货币）到教育（如远程学习）再到医疗（如2020年武汉抗疫），我们中的许多人仍会为此转变感到欣喜。

那么接下来的问题是，我们如何参与和引导科技建设一个更好、可持续的世界？

乌托邦或遗忘，进步或暂停，毕竟，未来只是我们每个人的明天。只不过这一天醒来时有人会满怀信心，有人会困惑地微笑，也有人会皱着眉头醒来。就像无数过去的日子一样，我们仍会在同一片天空下漫步，怀着敬畏又放松的心情穿越时间的河流，从不知不觉中溜走的分分秒秒中寻找意义。

未来，换言之，是由我们自己决定的。我们自主地决定做什么或不做什么。如今，随着数字技术的普及，无论是主动的还是被动的，如果没有某种科技服务于人以及科技与人的共生关系，我们的生活几乎是不可能继续的。而这些技术最终能做什么，仍然取决于我们自己。

我们和你们一样也非常关心，非常好奇，并且对未来充满信心。我们相信，只要有远见、勤奋、胆识和责任心，未来就能够更可持续、更高效、更方便、更包容。

无论你在罗马的竞技场还是北京的胡同，无论你是一名活跃的“数字游牧者”还是一个退休多年的老学究，我们都邀请你加入我们的探索之旅，一起想象明天对你我的日常生活意味着什么，我们如何运用科学进步改变我们的生活，同时也不忘时刻关注技术进步带来的负面效应。

读到这里，其实，未来就已经在你眼前了。

你准备好翻开“10个未来生活图景”了吗?

二

关于未来的十大生活图景

知乎 × Wavemaker

1. 未来的旅行

尽管对于越来越多的人来说，旅游已经成为他们生活中不可或缺的一部分，但近年来出现的大量应用技术——从在线旅行平台（OTA）到同声翻译功能，似乎并没有给人们的现实体验带来太多的改善。这主要是由于诸如原生语言与文化障碍，或时间限制而导致的其他困难所造成的，等等。结果，我们仿佛总是难以深入了解当地特殊性的人文历史、社会结构、风俗习惯，以致无法更好地贴近我们想要的真实。

我们的提问：旅行的终极意义是什么？而其边界仅在于时间、空间与文化吗？

畅想未来旅行的图景小故事

“世界是我的牡蛎”

——出自莎士比亚，意味梦想得以实现的世界

意大利，罗马

一位朋友曾经告诉我，独自旅行的美妙之处，在于可以享受未知中的自由选择，并能感受到那些未经雕琢的瞬间本质。

当飞机降落在这座世界历史古城上空时，我的“智能”眼镜开始放大划分整齐的乡村，向我展示不同产地葡萄庄园的葡萄品种——它似乎很了解我对葡萄酒的热情。我不觉得自己会有点惊慌失措，如果不是迫不及待地开始探索的话，反而感到了无法抑制的兴奋。

对于一个不会说意大利语的人来说，我的旅行包就是我的个性化指南——耳机开始忙碌地讲述着我走过的每一座宏伟的教堂和平凡店铺背后引人入胜可歌可泣的动人故事，我的眼镜同时捕捉到了这些点点滴滴，并为之标上了正确的路径。即使是在广场

上表演的街头乐手，智能眼镜也能告诉我，关于每首他们演奏的确切歌曲，还不忘提醒我记得给予掌声并留下小费。

在绕着古罗马竞技场走了一圈之后，我觉得这座古老的建筑——尽管它很宏伟极具代表性——已经不能满足我的好奇心了。坐在最上面一排安静的角落，我通过眼镜从网络云端选择了几个历史文件，点击下载，瞧！转眼间，就在相同的场景中，在我难以抑制的兴奋前，开始发生腥风血雨的生死搏斗、角斗士惊心动魄的玩命对决，被眼镜内置的AR功能毫无保留地将细节还原再现到了最后一刻。纵使以前在银幕上已经看过无数次类似的景象，环顾四周，在虚拟人物晦涩难懂的叫喊声中，我轻易地就能体会到古罗马人的原始与野蛮，他们的王公贵族弹指间就能无所顾忌地决定生死。突然间我感到深深的震撼，由衷感激自己出生在一个文明、和平的时代是多么幸运。

尝试了这段古老而刺激的体验之后，我决定找一家舒适日常的小酒馆解决午饭了。经过半个小时的考虑（他们看起来都很棒！），我最终决定走进一个仿佛处于迷宫中心的餐厅。多亏了我的眼镜，面前的意大利菜单立刻被翻译了出来，而服务员的友好问候在他说话的同时也被耳机翻译成了中文——尽管他意大利语的调调听起来比人工智能生成的中文翻译迷人得多！

回首这段旅程，正如我所预料的那样，这段一个人的旅行在任何时候都没有让我感到孤独。除了探索未知世界带来的自然乐趣外，我的高科技旅行包在一整天中都仿佛一个有灵魂的向导或知心朋友在指引我。有了它，“世界是我的牡蛎”，下一站要去哪里又有什么关系？

未来旅行趋势关键词

我们相信未来会出现：

时光机旅行

除了克服语言和文化障碍，尽情探索未知而不受限制，还要身入其中穿越古今！

借助人工智能提供的实时翻译和基于在地文化的提示，旅行者可以与当地人进行无障碍的交流，使他们能进一步深入当地文化的各个层面进行探索和挖掘。同时，基于实时定位（LBS）跟踪器记录下的旅程位置信息与总结，能为旅行者提供全面的安全出行保障。

虚拟虫洞

在时间和空间之间航行

身临其境的虚拟现实（VR）和增强现实（AR）技术使我们能够摆脱时空的限制，随时随地去感受。通过精密细致的交互功能，AR和VR用户可以仅通过观看历史或未来事件，就成为事件积极的参与者，并影响虚拟时间线的轨迹，而这种真实感甚至不亚于现实。

科技如何赋能未来？

结合LBS、智能识别、AR/VR、实时翻译等技术，5G和基于云计算的AI将能够为旅行中最常见的挑战提供解决方案，如沟通问题、文化障碍等，从而大幅提升旅行体验。

从这个角度来看，近年来迅速流行的应用程序，如移动AR表情符号、实时卫星导航和Pokemon Go，只能目前勾勒让我们看到一个更具互动性的未来。在成熟的5G网络以及沉浸式VR等当前新兴技术的支持下，它的存在跟发展势必将引领我们进入一个超越二维屏幕和线性时间线的世界，真正有着无尽无涯的结局。

哪些
是你想去，
但一直没有鼓起勇气
去的地方？

对未来旅行的乐观预期和发表有争议的评论

在未来，人们将获得哪些利益点？

更容易实现	随时随地旅行，可以避开疾病和时间短缺等物理限制
更有价值的经历	穿越时空，以更具互动性和沉浸感的设计参观不同的时间线和地点
更接近当地文化	更容易深入研究当地文化
更安全	全数字记录和跟踪，防止意外事故
更方便	无障碍沟通与理解
更易记录和回顾	永久数字化的旅行体验，深入最后一个细节，更容易重温珍贵时刻

同时，我们也会担忧：

当科技使旅行更方便的时候，当我们去一个从未接触过的地方时，我们所体验到的神秘感、未知的惊喜和喜悦会减少，甚至消失吗？“知之太多”会不会造成另一种流水线般出行的心态？

在任何地点、任何时间，沉浸式技术会让传统的以目的地为导向的旅游过时吗？

知乎上网友的脑洞提问：

人类如果要星际旅行，目前哪些问题还没有得到解决？应该怎么样解决？

如果真的存在时间旅行，为什么没有未来的人来到现在呢？

太空旅行在未来20年内会成为大众旅游项目吗？

乘上哆啦A梦里的时光机，你想穿梭去哪个时代？

地球上还会有哪些秘境等待我们去发现？

来自知乎上专家的提问：

栾方亮（Fred Luan）
澳大利亚旅游局，中国区市场总监
知乎ID：博多三号

我相信：未来的旅游就像空气和水一样，会成为生活不可缺少的必要部分。

- 未来会不会有任意门，从家里到目的地只需起身就能穿越？
- 未来的旅行会不会消除语言、文化、肤色的障碍，让人们得以闲庭信步，走近当地居民，融入当地文化呢？

- 未来的旅行者会不会更关注差异化的体验，而不是签到打卡、走马观花的旅行?

刘婷婷（Mona Liu）
马蜂窝旅游网 mafengwo.com，销售总监 Sales Director
知乎 ID：刘闹闹

我相信：世界奖励勇气大于奖励智慧.

- 未来太空旅行能否变得更加大众化?
- 未来旅行预订平台的角色会发生哪些根本性的变化?
- 未来会出现怎样的新型民宿?
- 20年后，人们会喜欢去哪里?

激发未来的商业和营销机遇：

商业启示

- 开发为旅行者提供便利的设备和工具，带来更方便流畅的旅行体验，如翻译工具以及在不同文化环境下的行为指导（如打招呼的方式、小费的给付等）；
- 借助AR/VR技术，开发目的地相关的内容和体验场景，给消费者带来更难忘的旅行体验；
- 开发更多可供虚拟旅行选择和内容，启发和帮助人们获得线上的旅游体验；

- 提供非侵入性隐私加密的追踪定位服务，以保障旅行的全程安全。

营销启示

- 在不同环境下识别不同消费者的出行动机与需求，准确构建系统性的沟通路径。例如，通过虚拟临场体验激发出旅行者对目的地的向往与渴望，根据旅行计划在关键时刻提供具有价值的相关产品，在实际目的地即刻辅助，激发用户更丰富的在地化体验感；
- 未来需要多方共同开发提升旅行体验的技术和内容，例如当代风云主题和历史人文故事情节；
- 未来会催生出更多类型的主题游和体验游，而不同行业的品牌将会成为重要的推动者，通过相关体验内容帮助消费者了解其品牌文化和价值观，产生深度共鸣与品牌信任度。

2. 未来的成长（1）——人才

当前产业结构的变化和新职业的出现，要求人力资源进一步多样化。其直接后果就是T型人才的崛起。与此同时，“刀耕火种”的一代和自由职业者正将一种多才多艺人才需求的大趋势推向主流，鼓励人们将个人选择融入职业规划，甚至创造出属于自己别于以往的全新工作。

由于新冠肺炎疫情的反复，“在家办公”变得前所未有地被重视及需要。要平衡快节奏的工作和生活，需要大大提高效率来维持。目前，无数的能提高效率的工具已经开始被公众广泛接受与使用。

与此同时，现有的高科技也开始释放我们在效率和创造力方面的潜力，使个人更加可塑和多元化。例如，人工智能滤镜技术，可以使每个人都能成为摄影专家，而人工智能写作和视频编辑技术，则为那些希望成为民间艺术家的人们，提供了更多展现艺术美感的表达机会。

我们的提问：未来的我们是否会实现更多的人生价值？那时的我们是否是快乐的？

畅想未来成长（1）——人才的图景小故事

自由切换多重职业，没人能规定我的“生涯”

一位新财经博主的来信：

作为一个财经新闻网站的编辑/视频博主，我喜欢和我的粉丝们分享财经知识和闲谈，无论是那些关于耸人听闻的时事评论，或是那些曾经熟为人知但已经被淡忘的故事。

一开始，我觉得做一个视频博客是很容易的——毕竟，其他博主的成功好像让这件事看起来很轻松。但当我开始录制和编辑我的第一段视频时，我突然意识到这是一个高度专业且要求苛刻的行业。不仅专业知识和不断研究的精神必不可少，还必须知道如何使用一系列视频编辑软件以及创意写作技能，将枯燥乏味、无法解释的事实转化为有趣的内容，并让不同的读者都能产生共鸣——至少能达成理解上的共鸣吧。当然，即便是上传一段模拟金融操作新手实操课程，也要在视频中体现共情，这会帮助视频获得更多的回应。好吧，现在你应该了解我在做的事情了。

幸运的是，我的朋友推荐给我了一款人工智能辅助应用程序，它非常令人意外地提高了我的创作效率。这个应用程序使用起来相当简单，我所需要做的就只是输入一个主题和几个关键字，点击红色按钮，然后以愉悦的心情将它发送。据我所知，这个程序会在云端筛选出难以想象的数据量，并在最终确定候选材料后，自动编写出初稿，方便我日后进行修改和扩展。而在视频处理方面，它从同一个云资源库中选取合适的图片和背景音乐，从世界各地的各类财经节目中剪辑节选，最后编辑成了一批最终的候选素材供我来选择。

不得不承认，这种人工智能的辅助大大节省了我原本投入的时间和精力。也许，专业团队也不过如此了吧。

这就是我的故事，一个单枪匹马成为视频博主的总结，希望对你能带来一些启发和鼓励。现在的我早已不再为有限的时间和资源而担忧，而对科技如何让我的工作变得更好抱有更大期待！

未来成长（1）——人才趋势关键词

我们相信未来会出现：

超π型人才

睿智通才+多领域专家

未来，在现有的职业种类中，大约有一半要么面临着被人工智能取代，要么会不复存在。随着传统劳务型的工作变得越来越稀缺，新的工种将应运而生。我们需要能够适应未来工作的不同要求。

因此，可能只有π型人才对于这种转变才更具适应性。π型人才指的是，既有广度（广泛的基础知识、多种专长和不同的能力）也有深度（高度特定的技能、对特定领域的投入等）的高级人才。

未来，需要有更高的工作效率的多面手。在技术进步的共同作用下，人们才可以腾出更多的时间和精力去做更有意义的事情。

科技如何赋能未来?

那些需要高度专业技能的工作，以及那些依赖于精确沟通、创造力和决策的工作，将成为主流的工种。人类将从重复的、劳动密集型的工作中解脱出来，例如数据收集和处理将被压缩或完全自动化。在效率工具和人工智能的帮助下，人们将能够在未来分配更多的时间，从事他们热衷的活动，更不用说人工智能还能帮助我们在个人爱好上有所提升，以至于我们可以成为这些领域的“专业人士”。

在创意方面，人工智能的潜力已经初见端倪：基于情感计算框架的人工智能系统“微软小冰”已经可以写诗作画；第一幅由人工智能创作的肖像画在佳士得拍卖行以43.25万美元成交；科幻作家陈楸帆的人工智能软件辅助小说在人工智能文学排行榜上获得了第一名……榜单还在继续。随着5G网络的遍地开花，人工智能艺术将继续扩展到更有创意的场所，这些场所需要更快的互联网和计算能力，比如视频流及平台。可以预见的是在未来3到5年内，人类和人工智能所共同制作的视频将变得更加流行酷炫。

同时，数字化正在加速内容产业的整合，而未来的云存储将大大提升数据通信的能力。此外，海量数据的爆炸式增长将导致现有服务器容量的不断升级，而基于5G网络的AI搜索功能，将进一步提高搜索引擎的准确度。

科幻作家/陈楸帆

我在2017年写《人生算法》这本书的时候就使用了AI协作来进行创作。有意思的是，虽然AI创造出来的句子没什么逻辑性，但读起来还挺美的。这些随机生成的素材给我带来新的写作灵感。

似乎拥有了更多的能力，便意味着更多创的可能性。如果可以变得超能，你想在未来能拥有什么“超能力”呢？

关于未来成长（1）——人才的乐观预期和带有争议性的评论

在未来，人们将获得哪些利益点？

工作更有效	以人工智能驱动的高效工具的普及
视野更开阔，体验更丰富	与不同领域的专家合作
更易成为领域专家	不断积累专业技能和经验
更多的职业选择	提供了更多的跨行业机会
人生更有目标	更好的职业目标规划
更具复合能力	多领域通才
更易获得成功	对所处领域抱有极大的热情

同时，我们也会担忧：

与人工智能技术进行顺畅互动和充分利用知识，是否会成为未来人群的基本技能？这种专业的通用语一旦通行，可以预见地能给社会提升效率和创造力，但对它的过度依赖会扼杀人类接下来的想象力吗？

随着个人偏好对职业生涯选择所起的决定性作用越来越大，是否会导致某些行业在人力资源过剩的情况下陷入一片红海，而使别的其他职业无人问津呢？

知乎上网友的脑洞提问：

未来精神和肉体发展的极限是什么？

当每个人都可以无所不能，人类会进一步追求什么？

如果可以选择三种超能力，你想要哪三种？

未来和算法、机器进一步融合后，人类的智力会有怎样的跃升？

来自知乎上专家的提问：

包益民（Imin Pao）
Vogue Business in China 编辑总监，PPGROUP & The Brand Partner 总裁
知乎 ID：IminPao 包益民

我相信：人们总是忙于为未来制订计划，而忘记了真正地活在当下。

- 如果你能回到20年前，并给自己一个建议，你会对自己说什么？

- 当你离开这个世界时，你希望别人怎样记住你？
- 如果你未来不需要以工作维生，你会做什么工作？
- 快，第一反应：你乘坐的飞机要坠毁了，你首先想到的是什么？
- 热爱一件事需要思考，爱情和疱疹有什么区别？

姜春鸣（Michelle Jiang）
群邑集团首席人才官 Chief Talent Officer, GroupM
知乎 ID：米米米

我相信：莫彷徨，未来已来。

- 未来，我们的社会需要什么样的人才？
- 未来，一个组织中的人才差异化会扩大还是缩小？
- 未来，新的年轻一代是否仍会拼搏和奋斗？

未来的商业和营销机遇：

商业启示

- 开发更好的效率工具与智能工具，提升工作效率、优化工作方法，助力人们更好地成为多面手，如AI拍照、剪辑和写作软件；
- 开发垂直或跨领域的人才合作和交流平台，为不同领域的专家创造更多的合作与交流机会，全面提升专业性，带来更多灵感和创造力；

- 鼓励多元领域的均衡发展，对缺乏人力资源的行业进行更具实际战略性的投资。

营销启示

- 针对提升多面技能的品牌和产品，进行基础的市场教育和沟通，帮助消费者获得更多的技能，例如沟通无人机的一键拍摄模式，帮助航拍入门者快速上手；
- 更精准地匹配不同类型的人才所需要的信息，尤其是更精准地匹配给垂直领域的专业人才，提供更专业的学习内容和交流机会；
- 透过数据和算法进行人才的发展预测，以激发其未来对新领域的增长与尝试；
- 将品牌转型为 π 型品牌，并与相应的人才进行沟通。这些人才不仅拥有相关行业的专业知识，而且在其他相关领域也有相当的潜力与知识。

2. 未来的成长（2）——学习

目前，虽然很多公（私）立学校和教育机构仍然采用传统的填鸭式教学和标准化的应试教育模式。但幼儿教育已开始慢慢转型，越来越多寓教于乐和多样化的学习内容与平台开始出现。它们开始将人工智能技术融入教学，根据学习效果，为学生匹配合适的课程。另外，教师们也在探索使课程更有趣、更鼓舞人心、更具影响力的新教育方法。

另一方面，由于新冠肺炎疫情的影响，远程学习模式——例如在线课程（实时或云计算）、“双导师”（在线+离线教师）等——得到了前所未有的普及，这些模式很可能在不久的将来成为主流。

我们的提问：未来的学习如何在由下而上的自我需求与由上至下的“必学内容”间获得平衡？必学内容，如文化传承、道德文明等知识。

畅想未来成长（2）——学习的图景小故事

虚拟演员和名人导演：一个跨越两个维度的场景

“这里演员的眼神再有感情一些。”

“这个镜头需要拉进一点。”

“演员和背景的对比需要再强化。”

轻轻一按开关，昏暗的房间里突然明亮了起来。在房间里，几个电影系的大二学生一整天都在来回踱步，他们在进行虚拟的拍摄学习与演练。

在他们全神贯注于拍摄的时候，人工智能导师已经对每个场景——从镜头角度、灯光，到实际表演——逐一进行了大量评论。而真实的授课教授正在对此详细阐述每一个不能被遗漏的细节。在这样一节典型的电影拍摄课堂上，每个学生都能得到关于他们作品的建设性反馈。

今天，他们重新拍摄了《花样年华》的结局。该课程使用了最先进的AI+VR全息人物模拟技术，通过进入一个拥有过去电影完整记录的演技数据库，精确模拟了电影中专业演员的神态动作（这是一个庞大的演员数据库，记录并能够模拟演员们的形象、风格、习惯等信息）。通过这一技术，学生们就可以亲手挑选自己理想的"虚拟明星"，而不用担心在拍摄个别项目时，找不到合适的演员。

这一次，当周慕云（虚拟版梁朝伟）问苏丽珍（虚拟版张曼玉）："如果多一张船票，你会不会跟我一起走？"的时候，苏还是那句最经典的台词："我会的"。

未来成长（2）——学习趋势关键词

我们相信未来会出现：

人性化体验式学习

适合个体需求与学习方式的体验式学习

- 真正的因人而异，因地制宜：针对学生的能力和兴趣领域不同，有相应的教育模式；
- 教育模式转型：填鸭式教育向沉浸式教育转变。科技赋能的体验式学习，启发思考、激励学习成为主流。

科技如何赋能未来?

未来，在人工智能的辅助下，学校教学和家庭辅导会变得高效且更有针对性。在学校，人工智能将会成为老师的左膀右臂，充当助教的角色。它能基于个人背景、兴趣和能力，为每个学生制订学习计划，甚至开发课程大纲，并匹配不同的教育资源；在家里，人工智能则成为虚拟家庭教师，为孩子提供完全个性化的辅导，并通过云端搜集最合适的教材，提供专门设计的相关课程。

未来几年，伴随高速传输和无延迟运算力的发展，VR的交互体验将越来越生动自然。VR的优势在于任意造景和仿真体验，除了应用于游戏娱乐领域，在教育领域的价值也不言而喻，尤其是当应用于危险性训练的教学及基础学科的普惠性教育时。未来，我们也许会从现在的云课堂衍生出云VR课堂，带来更沉浸式的个性化教学体验。

虚拟技术专家/L先生

VR技术的优势在于它不受传统物理因素的制约，是可以任意想象的。在教学中，它可以被用于救火、军事等带有潜在危险性的训练；也可以用于呈现极宏观或极微观的世界，比如宇宙、细胞。

教育创新咨询专家/Candy

强调体验式学习的PBL（project-based learning）其实成本很高，无法大规模普及应用；如果能通过VR沉浸式体验来学习，或许可以为个性化教育提供一个方向。

如果有专门为你定制的课程和沉浸式的教学环境，你还会觉得学习是一种压力吗？

关于未来成长（2）——学习的乐观预期和富有争议的评论

在未来，人们将获得哪些利益点？

学习更有乐趣	学习场景和内容更有趣，学习体验更丰富
学习更轻松容易	人工智能设备辅助教学，让学习变得简单
更加定制化	数据赋能和多样化工具与内容，实现因材施教
学习能力提升	利用科学手段和多样化的学习方式，来培养学生的思考能力
更易被启迪和激励	通过优化学习方式和教学手段，来启迪和激励学生

同时，我们也会担忧：

过度的定制是否会使我们彼此过于孤立，失去对“健康”学习至关重要的必要交流与相互激励？

过度依赖算法和外界刺激，是否会降低个体学习的主动性，降低学习的好奇心和创造力？

知乎上网友的脑洞提问：

如果可以在1天内学会一件很难的事，你最想学什么？

20年后，实体学校会消失吗？

来自知乎上专家的提问：

崔绮雯（Qiwen Cui）
知乎社会创新实验室 / 瓶行宇宙
知乎 ID：崔绮雯

我相信：未来基于我们的想象。

- 随着脑机接口等技术的发展，未来知识有可能直接“传输”而不用“学习”吗？
- 在未来，人工智能会成为我们的老师吗？

崔璀（Cui Cui）
优势大学（Youshi University）
知乎 ID：优势大学 Youshi University

我相信：未来是不确定的。只有一个人的优势，是稳定的，是你唯一的依仗，是这个不确定时代中的确定。

- 未来孩子们能从小就知道自己的先天优势吗?
- 未来人类获取知识的方式会发生哪些变化?
- 未来人类内心能否借助基因或者药物而变得强大?
- 未来人类的成长能否不受环境的影响?

未来的商业和营销机遇:

商业启示

- 无论线上还是线下，都需要更具有沉浸式的学习体验，如相关的平台、设备和内容，帮助人们在多场景和更多的感官刺激下，以趣味性和启发性的方式进行学习；
- 为不同的人、学生，不同的学习偏好、学习进度等，设计不同的教材和不同的学习方式，更好地帮助人们提升学习和思考的能力。

营销启示

- 让品牌助力教育，利用品牌在某一领域的专业度来帮助学生学习该领域的知识，使品牌在教育领域有更大的发挥；
- 教育无处不在，教育平台和内容成为品牌非常重要的触点和连接点。寻找品牌与教育类媒体合作的机会，设立品牌所在领域相关知识的课堂，或赞助相关的课程，来为品牌的宣传服务；

- 我们需要更好地利用人工智能和机器学习技术，更准确地确定个人偏好和潜力与能力及人格特质倾向，以便向消费者提供更有建设性与针对性的课程。

3. 未来的工作

2020年，全球为之震惊的新冠肺炎疫情毫无预警地到来，带来了许多不确定因素，透过此疫情也有了一些加速原先办公室工作的大规模形态转变，逐渐将办公室工作从传统的固定工作场所，重新定位到在家办公且更数字化，如运用数字科技领域进行相关会议、联系等。与此同时，许多公司开始尝试其他原先不同的工作模式，如弹性调配自主时间、在家工作等新的工作制度。

同时，随着可靠的互联网全面覆盖范围的扩大，加上计算机硬件和软件不断地优化更新，也使自由职业的机会在不可避免地逐步兴起。

我们也正在见证工作空间的快速转型，以共享的多用途工作区（如WeWork®）为例，其核心优势迎合了企业家和自由职业受众者日益增长的需求。因此，工作和家庭之间的传统界限，似乎更加趋于日益模糊。

我们的提问：在未来，工作的形态与方式将会有着如何颠覆性的改变？怎样的工作形态才是工作与生活平衡的最佳形态？

畅想未来工作的图景小故事

那就当个数字游牧民：因为工作是我的“一切”

Coco是一名人工智能领域的独立猎头和旅行博主，她喜欢和人打交道，也热爱旅游，对自己的现状非常满意。即使在直播她周游世界的旅行时，她也总是尽可能更多地会见当地的人工智能专家，丰富自己的资源储备。

彻底放飞那个曾受束缚的自己，沉浸一种游牧生活方式，这样的选择既让Coco乐在其中，但也给Coco带来了不少挑战。其中一个最初让她非常烦恼的，又特别难的挑战便是如何在日常、非专业的环境中，专注于手头的工作。为此，她找到了虚拟现实办公室。

通过戴上一副眼镜的简单动作，VR office可以通过显示多个语音控制或触摸激活的窗口，让她在视觉上重新定位到专业设置，只需简易的操作就能允许她编辑文档、流式视频、回复电子邮件和其他常见的办公活动。更好的是，全息会议室也可以在适当的条件下建立，使候选人和客户直接面对面交流，而不显示她所在的实际位置。

但Coco最近感到有点无聊，这是不可避免的，她一直在积极寻找新的项目，来保持自己的热情。经过一番简短的考虑后，她决定加入一个全球工作分享平台，这个平台除了配有标准的求职网站功能外，还可以把人工智能审核过的匹配项目的候选人定期发给她进行挑选。至于如何敲定这笔交易，自然是她说了算。

当每招到一个成功的新人，Coco都会按照自己的习惯，在猎头名单上加上另一个名字，更不用说那些结识新朋友的完美场合了，她现在高兴地称之为“一石三鸟”！

未来工作趋势关键词

我们相信未来会出现：

"随心所欲，自由切换"——工作生活一体化

工作伴随着生活，而生活则伴随着工作！

当今，"工作"与"生活"不再对立，它们正在相互和解，和谐相处。能够全身心地投身于深爱的事业，会使我们的幸福感倍增，也能让我们书写自己的未来故事。

数字游侠儿：跨时空的自由工作者

自由选择工作空间，规避传统的空间限制

除了更自由自在地选择工作时间和地点外，我们还可以更灵活地选择就业和团队的合作模式。

科技如何赋能未来？

随着自由职业者和 π 型人才的兴起，数字办公、远程办公以及虚拟办公将发展成为未来的主流趋势，这些工作的方式带来了许多好处，如降低成本、扩大空间限制、提高多任务与效率等。可以预见，随着我们越来越接近大规模远程工作的未来，我们也将面临一些挑战，例如如何促进实时通信和交流互动，或如何在办公室以外的自主协作环境，保持个人的专业和专注。随着技术的成熟、组织结构的演变，这一趋势可能还需要一定时间发展。

未来，除了虚拟办公以外，工作生活一体化下的我们还将需要生活、出行、职业规划等服务协同配合，从而让个体的人力资本潜能和时间价值得到最大化的释放。

因此，数字“游侠儿”将从日常生活的“僵化”中解放出来，取而代之的是，他们在生活和工作中有更多的时间和空间来变得更有创造力。

工作和生活之间的传统壁垒将不可避免地被推倒。到那时，你会努力只抓住原本那些熟悉的东西，还是大胆地接受这即将带来的新挑战？

关于未来工作的乐观预期和带有争议性的评论

在未来，人们将获得哪些利益点？

更容易获得就业机会	所有人，包含特殊人群、残障人士都能更容易找到适合自己的工作
更平衡，更快乐	工作与生活不再对立，在两者之间都能获得幸福感
更自由	工作的时间和空间，以及雇佣方式可自由选择

更高的工作效率	人工智能、大数据让工作分工更合理
更智能的资源分配	人才与合适的岗位进行更合理智能的匹配
人生更有掌控感	对生活有更好的管理和安排
人生更有成就感	热忱于激情更容易让人成功！

同时，我们也会担忧：

未来，制造业和服务业里的许多工作岗位，将被人工智能和机器人所取代。这将可能导致传统的劳务性质工作面临着相当大规模的消失，或许更紧迫的是，“失业”！这样的状况下，是否会增加人们的焦虑（担心将来工作被取代），更加降低现有生存价值的安全感吗？

工作由人工智能和大数据来调配虽然提高了工作效率，但也是否会带来一些负面影响（如时间被过于有效地安排、过度标准的工作模式和合作模式等）？

知乎上网友的脑洞提问：

5G 的出现会衍生出什么新型职业吗？

人工智能替代大部分工作后，还能剩下什么工作给人类呢？

未来会不会出现一种科技能够改变甚至主宰人类？

在工作和生活边界越来越模糊的未来，我们如何好好生活？

UBI（Universal Basic Income）全民基本收入可行吗？

来自知乎上专家的提问：

王佳（Vincent Wang）
百度，行业洞察总监
知乎 ID：王 Vincent

我相信：未来就藏在点滴的现在。

- 未来的人才是否可以避免被动地被“挑选”？而更主动去追寻生活的意义？
- 未来的公司组织会变成何种形态？机器人会是我的上级吗？
- 在赛博朋克的世界里工作，人们的心灵能否更好获得归宿感？

徐俊（Xu Jun）
伟达公关，中国区首席执行官
知乎 ID：XuJun

我相信：“未来已来”是要在现实中发现来自未来的讯息、获取灵感，抓住那稍纵即逝的、率先前往未来的船票。

- 未来的工作应该是那些需要灵感的工作，人类有灵感基因吗？能修复或增强吗？
- 智能机器人成为工作团队的重要组成，企业文化需要覆盖机器人吗？人类员工与机器人员工需要同工同酬吗？会出现机器人董事会成员吗？

- 人机联结、脑际联结技术能否让对工作的评估、反馈和辅导变得实时、心灵相通，没有延迟、情面障碍或者误读，而变得透明？

未来的商业和营销机遇：

商业启示

- 开发更适宜工作生活的空间与设施，如多元的办公空间和配套设施，使人们能更自由灵活地工作；
- 为自由职业者和数字游侠提供第三方协作平台，共享项目机会，让各类人才各司其职，共同合作，最大效能地发挥各自的作用；
- 施行去“中心化”的雇佣和工作的模式，利用AI和大数据，让工作分配更合理高效。

营销启示

- 在“工作生活一体化”的趋势逐渐催化人们注意力碎片化的态势下，将催生新的消费需求，改变既有的决策场景。营销人员需要捕捉和定义新的需求与场景，来设计相关的品牌与产品体验；
- 当工作场景与生活场景进一步融合，将重新定义人们的生活方式，以及触点的角色，尤其是工作相关的平台或媒介将在未来成为重要的沟通渠道；

- 品牌参与定义新的生活方式，将品牌的理念融入工作生活一体化的趋势中，并打造某种特有潮流。

4. 未来的娱乐

目前，关于“娱乐体验”，无论是在线流媒体还是视频游戏、逛街还是看电影仍然严重依赖于特定技术在某个场景空间上的体验，只能在某个场景或者某些条件下才能获得好的娱乐体验，比如更好的游戏设备、特定的时间段与更好的体验场所（如巨幕影厅）。

然而，随着沉浸式技术和科学技术（3D/4D、全息图、AR/VR、交互式电影）的普及，不久的将来，娱乐领域可能会为我们提供更充实、更容易获得的便民休闲体验。

我们的提问：在未来，娱乐还会是“娱乐”吗？而我们将仍是参与者还是获得娱乐体验的主导权？

畅想未来娱乐的图景小故事（1）

比分已定！

中午时分的CBD熙熙攘攘，办公楼下餐厅的一角，小纳和蝌蚪在一个拥挤的角落里，为昨晚的英超焦点大战争论不休。

“必须是点球，我确定看到了犯规。”小纳显然对他的球队那样输掉比赛感到不满！

“等一下，让我给你看看。”小纳拿出手机，找到了那个720度的现场直播视频片段，并将其减速至半速，“明白我在说什么吗？那家伙不是在背后拉他吗”？

“嗯，足球就是……你懂的，足球嘛。”蝌蚪耸耸肩，显然并不服气。

“嘿，这位同学，你在怀疑我的判断吗？”小纳笑了笑，看了看时间，同时，另一只手已经拿出他的VR眼镜了，接着说：“我们在球场上解决这个问题怎么样？”

"可以有!"蝌蚪拿出眼镜，踏踏地面，也兴奋了起来。

将智能眼镜连接到"FIFA 2030"游戏的云服务器上，并将手机设置为操纵器后，两位好友拉开了比赛的序幕。在这个午餐时间，虚拟的人群开始聚集在观众席上，就好像他们在昨晚那场非常刺激且耐人寻味的焦点大战中身临其境，并进行着第一人称的比赛——他们是全场的主角。

畅想未来娱乐的图景小故事（2）

怎么玩，我说了算

10岁的文杰，是一个十足的功夫迷。从李小龙、成龙到李连杰，还有甄子丹，如果你需要，他甚至可以将这些功夫电影明星的经典动作、台词及表情如数家珍地表演出来。文杰经常练习那些电影里的动作，他梦想着有一天他能亲眼看到自己挥舞着与明星们同样的拳脚招式与坏人进行伸张正义的搏斗。

幸运的是，他精通IT技术的父亲知道如何实现这个梦想。

为了给儿子一个惊喜，他把文杰带到了一家叫作"梦想重构"的媒体公司。这儿的服务宗旨就是为客户提供了与人工智能明星一起"行动"和飙戏的机会，而这些明星是从无数的电影数据中构建出来的。

完成了所有全息扫描后，一套触觉设备被用来记录文杰的武打动作——在空气中击打几下，再腾空跳跃十来下，人工智能就能直接进一步计算解构他的自然状态，创造出更精确、可信的模拟状态。

“一切都安排好了！”

在午夜的满月下，紫禁城之巅，文杰遇到了身穿武侠盔甲的“李连杰”。在传统武德的问候之后，两人都随即摆出自己师承宗派的功夫架势，对决开始了！整整3分钟，文杰左腾右挪，仿佛过江之鲫，而脸不改色的“李连杰”，接下了他全部的招式，并用一招“风林火山”化解了他凌厉的猛攻。过程极度真实。

“一切太酷了！”，当他们开车回家时，爸爸惊呼道，完整的视频片段已经传送到了他们的家庭云端，文杰在狂喜中将视频分享到了他所有的社交媒体账户上，立马向全世界得瑟自己的表现。

此时，文杰的爸爸却似乎有些按耐不住。他忽然萌生了个念头：我是不是可以和奥黛丽·赫本来一场

“纽约假日”呢？

在他的脑海里，他已经能看到奥黛丽·赫本，华丽，辉煌，优雅。她轻轻地挽着他的胳膊，在海边散步……

未来娱乐趋势关键词

浸入与否

随时随地畅快连接、浸入感官式的体验

未来，随着5G、6G等技术的发展和普及，连接的体验将得到飞跃式的提升，可以随时随地都拥有高流畅度、高清晰度的连接。同时，我们希望未来能够实现跨平台与设备的互联（比如游戏设备间的互联），打破连接的障碍。而未来，沉浸式体验也将得到进一步的提升，比如更立体、更多维，以及多视角的感官体验。无疑，这将进一步打开你的感官，但无人能预测在感官长期暴露在浸入式刺激下，会给人类带来什么。

情感沉浸

不做旁观者！成为参与者与主角，创造属于我的娱乐体验

我们不再仅仅是音乐、电影、游戏或其他以叙事为中心的娱乐活动的旁观者。相反，在互动设计的帮助下，我们可以积极参与，甚至作为主角，参与到故事的创作中来。我们还可以自己来决定获得什么样的娱乐体验，如选择电影的另一条故事线或结局，或者与某位知名影星共同演绎某个桥段。

未来，科技是如何赋能的？

未来高速网络的传输速度足以让我们体验到超高清、流畅的在线视频和线上游戏；云存储和云计算可以让我们抛开存储介质的束缚，随时随地进行游戏互联。

同时，辅以AI和AR/VR、动作捕捉和3D模拟等开创性技术，娱乐体验将实质性地变得更具沉浸感。

另外，我们还将真正“主宰”我们的娱乐，通过选择更适合自己的体验（比如观感与视角），甚至参与或进入体验的内容（比如选择游戏或电影的不同情节或者结局、自己成为故事的主角等），我们将在掌握自己的娱乐休闲体验上获得更多的“上帝视角”。

未来的你希望怎样主宰自己的娱乐体验？

关于未来娱乐的乐观预期和带有争议性的评论

在未来，人们将获得哪些利益点？

感官体验更沉浸	更多视角，更立体化
能掌控的体验	自己决定内容和视角
更随心所“娱”	游戏设备可随时随地互连
更有趣味性	故事性的内容，多样化的体验
更有参与感和创造性	“我”是内容的主角或裁判

连接更流畅	高流畅度、高清晰度的体验
人生充满乐趣	生活娱乐化

同时，我们也会担忧：

未来娱乐的无障碍性与浸入性是否会削弱我们的感官，并将我们推向更加极端化的娱乐追求？

过度娱乐化而造成的沉溺现象是否会变得更严重？

知乎上网友的脑洞提问：

未来世界的生活是否会像《黑客帝国》展示的那样？

未来，虚拟偶像会取代真正的明星吗？

假如人类在虚拟游戏《我的世界》中生存和发展，1 000 年后世界将会怎样？

两个能预知未来并且都想赢的人，玩剪刀、石头、布，谁会赢？

当“虚拟”成为“现实”，我们如何更好地游走在两个世界？

来自知乎上专家的提问：

王宇航（Eric Wang）
腾讯，创作者增长
知乎 ID：tiao-deng-kan-jian-65

我相信：未来科技可以替代物理人力，但无法取代情感交互。

- 未来的娱乐将更多发生在现实的世界还是虚拟的世界？未来的人们是否可以选择永久沉浸在虚拟的世界？
- 在未来，娱乐的快感是否会超出人类的感知临界点？
- 内容承载、传递的最终形式是什么？
- 未来的内容将会由少数人创作还是多数人创作？

王博霖（Ken Wang）
品牌营销咨询，星美集团前营销负责人
知乎 ID：kk-wang-27-26

我相信：未来，足不出户便可畅游全宇宙！

- 如果真有时光机，是否哆啦A梦会更早问世？
- 怎样界定未来娱乐可能涉及的法律约束与执法界限，以及如何防止道德越矩？
- 未来的娱乐，是否会更加由虚拟游戏或想象为主导，再打造出真实的环境与场景？
- 娱乐是否会被重新定义？人们是否能从个体与群体的行为组合中收获最大的快乐？

未来的商业和营销机遇：

商业启示

- 在高速网络的发展下，借势5G甚至是6G的运用，为用户提供更快速和稳定的娱乐服务；
- 提供更通畅无阻的互连支持，使玩家随时随地随心连接不同平台的好友，进入不同的游戏世界；
- 提供多感官（视觉、听觉、嗅觉、触觉等）的沉浸式娱乐体验（尤其是基本的娱乐形式，如游戏、观看体育赛事、欣赏音乐会）；
- 让消费者更有参与感，让消费者参与到产品和内容的设计环节，共创体验。

营销启示

- 推动品牌参与到构建人们娱乐生活的过程中，无论是产品设计、广告内容、线上线下互动，定义好品牌在娱乐生活中应当承担的角色；
- 娱乐营销更沉浸化，会催生出更多更具故事性和互动性的传播方式和内容，品牌应设计符合“由下至上”的内容创造机制；
- 挖掘和识别消费者不同的娱乐需求与场景，通过更具沉浸式的平台、设备和内容，来精准设计和建立深度的品牌体验。

5. 未来的消费

传统零售已经开始向智能化、体验式零售转型，但由于技术等方面的限制，仍有很大的发展空间。因此，当今的所谓的新零售、数字体验店可以说噱头有余，升级不足，整体购物体验与传统零售相比并没有多大的改变。

但我们也要看到积极的一面，尤其在电商领域，如淘宝的“千人千面”功能，利用大数据和算法为不同的消费者推送不同的商品和广告。这是一个好的开端。

我们的提问：未来，我们如何平衡理性与感性，做出最具价值的消费判断？

畅想未来消费的图景小故事

巴黎政变

在一家复古香水店里，一部惊悚片正在上演。

一声枪响，打破了无月之夜的宁静。

枪声的回响蜿蜒地穿过巴黎静谧夜空下那空无一人的小巷，从像哨兵一样矗立的街灯旁摇曳而过。因刚刚下过雨，湿漉漉的街灯在午夜的薄雾中散发着夜的气息，在鹅卵石路上显得格外苍白。

一个寂静的身影掠过街道，后面追赶着几个打着手势的警察。他们正在把那个逃亡的影子赶进了死胡同。

似乎就要成功了，他们包围了那条浅浅的巷子，有点犹豫着要不要跨过那摇曳的光明和永恒的黑暗之间的，那条诡异的界线。警察们疲倦地互相眨着眼睛，好像在争论谁该先走。突然，出乎大家意料的是，从几英尺外的无光角落里，走出一个年轻女子。她穿着一件无可挑剔的黑色晚礼服，戴着一副同样颜色的天鹅绒手套，嘴唇上涂着灼热的胭脂红，眼睛里闪烁着翡翠色的光亮，仿佛被猫的灵魂附身了。在她看似大理石般温润的脖子上，不经意地挂着一条美丽绝伦的宝石项链。上面是博物馆刚刚报告丢失的那颗无价钻石。

这位女子带着谦虚又腼腆的微笑，轻快地从这排目瞪口呆穿制服的警察——这些人仿佛石化了一般——身边走过，消失在另一个街角。空气中挥之不去的是她身上残留的痕迹，那是一种盛开的曼陀罗的迷人香味，优雅得让人无法抗拒，甜美得令人窒息。

场景如定格画面般，一个接一个地闪过。在阴云密布下的神秘小巷中，像街灯般呆立着的警察们从这个只可意会不可言传的梦境中回过神来——所有的一切都消失了。

这时全场大灯亮起了，眼前的仍旧是刚刚那家复古香水店内部陈设。刚刚发生的一切似乎都不存在。然而，空气中却弥漫着刚刚那女子身上醉人的香气，久久不能散去。

事实证明，这场秀是该店最新的线下快闪活动的一部分，旨在通过定制内容推广更好的沉浸式购物体验。很显然，它再次让人们陶醉。在一大群热情洋溢的顾客中，一个年轻女子扭动着身子走到柜台前，带着仍然显而易见的兴奋问道:“劳驾，请问那是什么香水?”。

“这是我们的‘反转巴黎’,”一个微笑的年轻人回答,“最迷人的是它的中后调，也就是您刚才闻到的味道。”女孩不假思索，立刻购买了这款香水。拿到的包装上，还印着一个浅浅的红色唇印。

她盯着这个唇印，眼前仿佛浮现了刚才黑衣女郎款款走过的身影。她捧着香水，脸上挂着灿烂的笑容，爱不释手地走出了店门。

未来消费趋势关键词

一千个人，一千个哈姆雷特

个人化、定制化、更高效的购物体验

通过身份识别技术和大数据分析，在店铺设计、商品陈列方式、招待服务等方面，为消费者提供更符合他们兴趣喜好的定制化购物体验，或偶尔非常特殊的偏好和需求。

与传统消费相比，这种360度定制体验的效率要高得多，特别是通过减少不匹配产生的浪费来积极促进可持续消费。

很可能会有更多类似的方法，能更充分地利用成熟的数据技术来指导消费者做出有意义的决策。

玩乐买买买

体验式零售，启发式选择

传统线下零售在科技的赋能下向多元化转型，提供更多样、新型的购物体验：如剧场式购物、主题派对式购物、展览主题购物等，从而激发和满足消费者的好奇心。与此同时，零售场所还可以提供现场娱乐，同时作为一个影响和引导消费者发现激起他们不同兴趣的趋势的地方。

未来，科技是如何赋能的?

在可预见的未来，消费者对个性化产品和服务的追求将演变为对定制化购物体验的需求。在线下零售商中，大数据将被广泛用于提供高度定制的服务。线下店铺将更细分化，会根据特定偏好对关键人群进行划分，并辅以定制的感官和互动设计、具有针对性的沟通，让消费者感受到——这里是一个真正属于“我”的消费空间。

与此同时，线下购物将具有更多功能性。现在，人们对于线下购物的需求已经不再是买东西那么单一了，在购物中体验娱乐、艺术、潮流、时尚，将会是一种全新的生活方式。比如在消费者购物过程中，加入通过激光全息技术实现的全景仿真体验环节，会大大增添购物的乐趣，同时在仿真体验的过程中对产品进行植入宣传，也能极大增强消费者对产品利益点的感知度。

你是哪个品牌的忠实消费者？如果你是这个品牌的CMO，你希望在五年后给消费者创造怎样的品牌体验？

关于未来消费的乐观预期和带有争议性的评论

在未来，人们将获得哪些利益点？

更具多元体验性	集娱乐性和实用性于一体的多元品牌体验
更高效的供应链	从消费到生产，再从生产到消费的效率提升
更具启发性	通过多元场景和内容，启发消费者追求更美好的生活
选择更容易	有更相关的信息，帮助消费者做决策
更定制化	商品界面、陈列、服务的高度定制化

同时，我们也会担忧：

习惯性地依赖于算法建议的消费选择是否会把我们推入信息的茧房，形成“消费孤岛”现象，不可逆转地缩小我们的视野？

向体验式消费的转型是否会使理性决策边缘化，并引发更多的冲动消费？

随着数字化趋势的进一步发展，某些品类的实体商品将会渐渐消失，而某些具有文化和时代象征的商品是否也会消失呢？

知乎上网友的脑洞提问：

实体门店还有未来吗？

直播带货还能火多久？未来趋势会怎样？

可持续产品，是未来的新消费主义吗？

来自知乎上专家的提问：

王婧（Jing Wang）
胖鲸 SOCIAL ONE, Founder and Chief Knowledge Officer
创始人兼首席知识官
知乎 ID：DizzyWhale

我相信：对未来真正的慷慨，是把一切都献给现在

- 当技术和数据能帮助品牌越来越了解消费者，甚至能帮助消费者越来越了解自己时，消费是否会变得越来越理智？还是更加注重情感价值？

黄勇（Young Huang）
慧辰，公共事务部总经理
知乎 ID：Young

我相信：处变，有持

- 在未来，禁忌的魔盒是否会被打开？比如，你是否会给孩子植入提高智商的芯片？你是否会因为担心疾病而希望修改孩子的基因。
- 线上消费对线下消费几乎带来了颠覆性的影响，未来颠覆线上消费的可能是什么模式？

未来的商业和营销机遇：

商业启示

- 基于历史数据分析，预判消费者需求，更主动地提供高度定制化的产品或服务。无论是线上线下店铺的设计、选品与沟通方式，还是售后服务，都需要满足消费者个人化的需求；
- 根据消费者的需求进行生产和资源调配，提高整个供应链的效率；
- 通过打造新的应用场景，来激发消费者对于提升生活品质的想象。

营销启示

- 在消费者路径的重要环节叠加多元体验（如全息投影产

品演示以制造兴趣、推动转化等），帮助消费者在消费决策路径上丰富品牌体验，提升营销效率；

- 更好地利用营销科技进行需求和场景的识别，并匹配针对性、更有价值的信息，启发和缩短消费决策路径；
- 设计更多维体验的零售模式、促进跨界/产业的合作，为品牌打造更多元的零售功能和体验；
- 品牌是打造新型消费体验的弄潮儿，品牌应以自己的属性和特色为基础，大胆尝试打造发挥品牌价值的场景体验。

6. 未来的家庭

目前，我们的家已经开始承担更多的功能性需求，比如娱乐和办公的需求。这一趋势在新冠肺炎疫情后变得更为明显。这种可能不安的突发性转变，也催生了更多智能家用设备的普及，比如清洁扫地机器人和语音控制的家电用品。与此同时，在安全照护方面，无论是在室内还是室外，定位跟踪、监控老人及儿童的智能设备，也正被越来越多的家庭所接受和应用。

我们的提问：未来，何以为家？

畅想未来家庭的图景小故事

温柔地，入夜

晚上8点30分，我计划了一个月的“VR焰火秀”如期而至，这一个月的研究、设计，再到最后一个细节的检查都是值得的。它，照亮了我在的五楼公寓里的虚拟天空。

20年前，在明静的夜空下，我和妻子无可救药地坠入爱河。然后，我们结婚了！

20年后，当夏日的太阳毫无保留地将光芒投向大地时，我们慵懒地躺在床上，试图从头顶上盛放的每一朵烟花间，细细回味属于两人共有的回忆，那些一同走过的酸甜苦辣。

天色渐暗，绚丽的烟花被投射在窗外一方小小的夜空中。我们躺在床上，听着窗外令人兴奋的烟花声，我侧过头看到她的眼睛，那里正藏着花火映射下的美丽光芒。我温柔地看着她，她的肌肤流动着温润而年轻的光泽。当我正在思考应该怎么去形容她的美，她侧过头，像往常一样很不自信地问："我是不是老啦？不再好看了吧？"我摇摇头说："你永远这么漂亮。"停顿了一下接着又说道："真的，真的很漂亮！"然后我转过身将她整个人深深地拥在怀中，我喜欢这样贴近她、亲吻她。如此熟悉的味道、触感和温度，纵使在这烟火喧嚣的夜晚，此时此刻，我的内心突然有一种特别的平静。

"想我了吗？"她轻轻地问。我点点头："想，想极了！"她低下头，再抬起头时，我隐隐看到她眼里的泪光，"我也想你！"

我点点头，不停地点头。

她转过身，将柔软的身体缩在我的臂弯中。随后，她的身影如像素般逐渐消融——就像昨天的阳光，化为今天的虚无。

5年前，在我们结婚15周年纪念日那天，在没有月亮的天空下，她观看了一场烟火表演，回到家中，她离开了我。终成为我不想醒来的梦。

未来家庭趋势关键词

家 +

集多元功能于一身的家

随着工作与休闲的逐渐融合，未来的家将是一个工作、娱乐、学习、社交、育儿等的多功能场所。

智能家属

无微不至的智能管家

随着智能家居、物联网的不断发展，家居生活将变得更智能、便捷，它会识别家人的不同需求和情绪并提供解决方案。所有家庭成员甚至宠物都可以得到实时的健康管理和照料护理。而“它”的存在，将如电影里那般作为“家庭”的一部分而存在。

未来，科技是如何赋能的?

被智能家居设备和可穿戴设备包围，无疑会让日常生活变得更轻松、高效。如果说完成基本工作是智能设备发展的第一步，那么我们很可能会在未来几十年见证快速、实质性的进展，这将使已经有着智能设置的设备真正智能化。在物联网和机器学习技术的推动下，未来的家庭设备不仅能够自主学习，适应不同家庭的特殊性，甚至可能在某些能力上变得有知觉，为每个成员提供个性化的服务。这将逐渐改变智能家居的前景，从依赖独立的、单一用途的设备，到由设备间的“群体智能”驱动的多用途连接。

目前，人工智能和全息技术仍然是相互独立的。然而，目前的趋势表明，两者的融合是不可避免的。通过高速互联网，未来我们将能够与全息管家交流——就像我们彼此之间的交流一样——他们几乎在各个方面都可称得上是完美的“人类”。

高级数字体验设计师/林居颖

在我看来，智能思维的发展分为三个阶段：自然、自主、自适应。自然，意味着在设定范围的交互上“像人”而不是机器；自主，是从被设定的范围和条件到主动自学习的能力；而自适应，意味着可以灵活适应多变的场景。

当科技可以感知你的内心甚至抚慰你的心灵，你是否还愿意对他人敞开心扉？

关于未来家庭的乐观预期和带有争议性的评论

在未来，人们将获得哪些利益点？

让每个人都更舒适	会识别家人的不同需求和情绪并提供解决方案，让每个人都能享受舒适的家居生活
获得更多适合自己的生活建议	为你的生活出谋划策，比如穿着、饮食或生活方式等
更安全	应用带人脸识别系统的门禁系统、高清且能与移动设备互连的监视设备
获得更多自由时间和轻松感	最大程度地将人从家务劳动中解放出来
更多功能	集工作、娱乐、学习、社交、亲子等的多功能场所
更多新鲜感	科技让人们随心所欲地改变家装风格
生活更井井有条	未来智能系统会扮演更多家庭管家的角色
能够关爱每一位家庭成员	老人、孩子和宠物的实时照护

同时，我们也会担忧：

全面数字化和网络化，是否会对家庭财产和隐私安全产生威胁？

未来，负担得起高科技产品和服务的人是否会获得更美好的家庭生活，这是否会进一步拉开人们生活品质之间的距离，而加深社会阶层问题？

知乎上网友的脑洞提问：

你理想的家庭生活是什么样子的？

在未来，住宅的发展趋势和设计思路可能会是怎样的？

未来30年或更长久的可预见未来，中国家庭结构模式会有怎样的变化？

随着持续的工作生活的融合，未来理想的“家”会是什么样的？

未来会有哪些方式，让家庭的关系更美好、和谐？

来自知乎上专家的提问：

张若玥（Dorothy Zhang）
WonderHouse 联合创始人，未来的"人生何去何从"探索者
知乎 ID：桃乐丝的清晨

我相信：掌控万物，是晋级，也是欲望扩张，不忘敬畏与反思

- 未来的家庭除了夫妻（+孩子），还会有哪些不同的形式？
- 你希望自己的老年阶段在怎样的家庭内部和外部环境中度过？
- 人离世后，能够以哪些形式和深爱自己的家人互相陪伴？
- 未来家庭成员间的链接主要靠什么维系？
- 智能家居用品的普及，会让我们的机能退化吗？

吕妍（Louise Lv）
飞利浦（中国）投资有限公司，数字化中心负责人
知乎 ID：丽莎

我相信：未来的生活会更便利，沟通会更顺畅，社会分工也会更细致且专业化，但同时也可能会更圈层化和小众化。

- 未来家庭成员的沟通会更紧密还是更疏离？可能因信息孤岛效应和圈层文化越拉越大的代际鸿沟，会怎样影响家庭成员间的关系？

- 在未来，长辈的经验/知识是否可以通过芯片/数据来传递给下一代？
- 今后智能化会否渗透到每个生活场景？比如智能冰箱能可视化/菜单化所有事物的列表、存放天数、生成菜谱，一键下单配送到家。
- 由于数据和科技的实现，是否会促使人们享受舒适的生活而不愿尝试改变？

李爽（Sabrina Li）
Lead8，主任设计师
知乎 ID：林不爽

我相信：未来会更好

- 未来的家庭需要通过婚姻来定义吗？
- 在未来的家庭生活中，幼童和老人会得到怎样的关注和关爱？
- 未来的收入会不会考虑以家庭为单位，而不是以个人为单位？
- 未来衣食住行等资源可以怎样被更好地平衡，并缩短贫富差距？

未来的商业和营销机遇：

商业启示

- 设计开发更智能的家居产品或系统，精确识别家人不同心理和生理需求，提供适合的解决方案以及灵活的功能与空间组合，使每个人都能享受到舒适的家庭生活；
- 进一步提升家居生活的效率，如更多的解放双手或提高效率的居家工具，让人们从烦琐的家务中解放出来，获得更多的自由时间；
- 开发更进阶的安保设备和监护设备；另外，针对家庭网络和家庭成员个人数据，可以推出相关防火墙产品或服务，来预防未来的网络犯罪。

营销启示

- 清晰定义不同品牌与解决方案在家庭生活中的角色和定位，帮助品牌更好地融入消费者的家庭生活；同时，也需要更好地促进不同品牌的合作，设计综合性的沟通方案；
- 针对不同的家庭成员，匹配个人化的沟通内容与解决方案，例如为每位家庭成员提供更贴心的生活建议；
- 更准确地识别家庭设备的用户以及场景，如多个家庭成员在一起的欢聚时光，用户与场景切换等，精准地匹配适合该家庭成员与场景的沟通内容。

7. 未来的社区

目前，大多数中国社区仍然是以居住为主要功能的住宅小区，其设计目标是住房，而更多的社会生态可持续社区远未成为主流。

一个未来社区的雏形可以用上海五角场地区来举例：这是一个大规模的综合社区，从教育、食品零售、医疗，到工作和娱乐都融为一体。

我们的提问：未来的社区是否会帮助实现生活本应拥有的样子？

畅想未来社区的图景小故事

虚拟的麻将，真正的朋友：生态社会社区一瞥

70岁出头的老张在一开始的时候，打心眼儿里是反对搬到新建成生态社区的。“这些年轻人就是不明白‘邻居’到底是什么意思！”每当有人提起这个话题，他都会提出疑问。

作为一个退休多年的老教授，老张很难想象那种传统的居住社区之外的生活，也从来没有想过要告别曾经漫长而刻骨铭心的岁月。对老张来说，在早上慢跑回家的路上偶遇熟悉的面孔，下午和老同志们打几局麻将或下棋，几乎等同于一切美好。当他第一次听说城市另一边的那些新开发的社区时，那种被描述成童话般的便利（一站式服务站无处不在——啊？那么可以想象！以后谁还需要邻居呢？！），每每想到这里，他总是会挥起表示反对的手臂。

但敌不过女儿连续两年的软磨硬泡，老张耸耸肩，

举起了白旗。在搬家那天，老张有些低落。他知道这可能是不可逆转的失败，甚至能听到从汽车后座传来“年轻人真的不懂社区是什么”。

把老张安顿好后，女儿和女婿中午就离开了，他们有半天的工作要赶。看着这对离去的夫妇，身后的门自动缓缓关上，老张在他曾祖父传下来的老式餐桌旁坐下。他扶了扶眼镜，眯着眼睛看着客厅另一边那面空当当的米白色的墙，一时陷入了沉思。

“我本来可以用……来结束那盘棋的，”在思考的时候，门铃意外地响了，打断了刚刚的咕哝声。

外面站着两个微笑的年轻女子。她们看起来还算和善，老张心里想。尽管如此，他意识到自己还是有些怀疑地盯着她们，尽管只有几步之遥。

“你一定是张先生，我们的新住户，”右边的人轻声说道，显然是想打破僵局，“我是简因，这是朱莉，我们是社区中心的。你介意我们进来带你参观一下吗？这个地方可能看起来有些空荡荡的，但里面可是满满的智能设备，只是你需要一些时间去适应它们”。

“好的，请进，那麻烦你们带我看看吧。”老张让出空间让她们走过去，其间略显尴尬地笑了笑，他有些担心是否她们要把在女儿家看到的那些没用的

“垃圾”卖给他。

朱莉在桌边坐下，拿出一副眼镜，看上去和老张鼻子上的眼镜没什么区别。

“这是我们社区开发的智能眼镜，您想试试吗?”难以推辞下，老张换上了朱莉的眼镜。“眼镜需要一两秒钟才能适应你的眼睛状况，所以如果你看到到处都是模糊的东西，请不要害怕。”正如朱莉所说，他的视力从1个模糊的小点在1秒钟后就开始聚焦。“现在好些了吗?”

“是啊。是啊。孩子，这真了不起”，老张心想，试图去想起他最后一次这样清楚地能看到东西是什么时候的事。

“太好了。现在，除了定制的视力，它还会连接到互联网，以及你家里的一切——它会对你的语音指令做出反应，”简因补充道，“例如，如果你想要一份特定的报纸，只要说出报纸的名字，它就可以读给你听。”

这一切似乎让老张感到有些上头。他试着向四处望去，以前空无一人的地方突然贴满了纸，每一个贴纸上都有简洁而详细的说明。

“如果你不想自己读，你也可以让它读给你听，比如报纸。”看到他微微点头，朱莉接着说：“我们在每栋楼的一楼都有一站式服务站，有任何需求都可以去咨询——如果你不想走下楼，只要跟眼镜说，我们马上就把它们送到。”

“这栋楼旁边也有一家社区医院，如果你觉得有需要的时候，请告诉我们，”简因轻轻地敲了敲眼镜，“我们会尽快请一位全科医生或专家过来。”

简因话音未落，老张的眼镜就发来一个高分贝的提醒，吓了他一跳。“这可能是你的朋友在你之前搬过来的，他们正在连线你。如果你想接受他们的请求，只要点头就可以了。”

老张按照指示点点头，让他惊讶的是，这正是他的朋友老李，几个月前搬走的那个老李。

“老李！怎么回事？我不记得看到你进门了呀！”

“谁说我来了？”老李笑着解释说，这是一个虚拟通话，跟真的一样！“如果你不想出去”，老李继续说，“让我下次打电话给老方和老孙，咱们来几圈虚拟麻将，就跟以前一模一样，就像面对面一样！”

两个女孩儿在带他参观了新家的半个小时就离开了。老张戴着眼镜走出门外，眼镜从鼻梁上滑下来，他回头看了看那虚假的空虚，然后微笑着慢慢地把眼镜推了回去。

也许，这一切可能并没那么糟。

未来社区趋势关键词

我们相信未来会出现：

社区生态化

多功能化和社会生态可持续的中心社区

社会生态化：

- 更多样功能与协同：医疗、照护、工作、教育、购物、生活服务、社交平台等；
- 健康生活的管理体系。

去围栏效应：

- 住宅社区不再作为独立单元被管理，而是融入更开放边界的社区，更充分地利用和共享硬件与软件。

科技如何赋能未来?

目前，社区发展基本上停留在对现有功能的优化或升级上。在未来，社区将以满足人们美好生活向往为根本目的，通过将目前不相连的社区合并成新的住宅区，从而重塑社区生活，围绕社区全生活链服务需求，以人本化、生态化、数字化为价值导向，通过邻里、教育、健康、创业、建筑、交通、能源、物业和治理等场景的创新，重塑整个城市景观，成为引领未来生活方式变革的新型城市功能单元。除了提供方便、可靠的基本社会设施外，还将采用更可持续的管理策略，以确保当地生态系统的完整性。

持续的数字化趋势将进一步使未来的社区具有内置的高科

技连接，由大数据、5G、物联网、智能可穿戴设备等实现。因此，这将使得传统的自上而下的社区规划模式演变为横向管理驱动的社区运营模式（志愿服务、承担公民责任等），考虑到每个社区成员的需求。

此外，这种横向管理的模式将使社区作为社会生态单元更加自我维持，提高社区弹性，从而有效缓解城市管理压力。

未来的多功能社区是否会提供无处不在的自动化一站式服务，让你在社会上更加独立（更宅）？

关于未来社区的乐观预期和带有争议性的评论

在未来，人们将获得哪些利益点？

更宜居更可持续	居民与当地生态系统的可持续关系
更便捷	更多元功能与协同：医疗、照护、工作、教育、购物、生活服务、社交平台等
更有韧性	运用社区自组织的力量更好地应对突发公共危机
资源共享	共享不同社区的资源，不同社区可以共同发展与提升

更有人文气息	文化创意产业园等带来的文化和社会活动更加丰富
更开放的交流和互动	社区无边界，帮助不同社区的人们更好地沟通、交流与互动

同时，我们也会担忧：

社区社会生态发展的潜在倾斜是否会导致资源分配的不平等（例如好的资源，如医疗、教育资源向高档社区倾斜）？

在很大程度上，自动化和集中的社区设施，再加上互联网服务的便捷性，是否会削弱人们的社交意愿，缩小活动半径，产生生活上的“孤岛效应”呢？

知乎上网友的脑洞提问：

未来10年，我们的社区生活会因科技发生怎样的变化？

未来，共享“共居”会是一种主流形态吗？

你希望未来居住的社区，有哪些更好的公共空间？

现在很缺少邻里关系和文化，未来会改变吗？

来自知乎上专家的提问：

胡镔（Bin Hu）
未来学家俱乐部，联合发起人
知乎 ID：binhu87

我相信：未来不可预测，只待创造！

- 人与人的心理距离会变得更近还是更远？
- 母系社会会重新回到人类的视野吗？
- 在未来，血缘关系会消失吗？
- 未来会出现一个完全以兴趣为关系纽带的社会吗？
- 在火星上，我们会如何改造我们的社会结构？

谭亚幸（Jacob Tan）
MSC 咨询联合创始人 &CEO
知乎 ID：Jacob

我相信：富人靠科技，穷人靠变异？

- 幸福感会越来越难获得吗？
- 冰川融化，不断压缩的物理生存空间会带来全新的斗争吗？
- 消费会更基于信任（情感纽带）还是基于事实（客观数据）？
- 离数字奴隶出现还有多远？
- 平权与多元化的话语体系会如何不断进化？

未来的商业和营销机遇：

商业启示

- 社区间和社区内的联系有助于将社区空间转变为独特的社会生态系统。最重要的是，未来的企业要学会适应这种转变带来的潜在需求；
- 各产业需要发生更大的协同效应，与政府的资源进行配合，共同打造多元功能的社区。同时，通过科技手段将社区各项功能进行连接，为社区居民提供一站式的解决方案；
- 基于社区的特点、所在的城市与地域文化，打造具有特色的社区，从而吸引更相关的群体与商业主体带来更健康的社区发展。

营销启示

- 未来将发展出更多样化的、基于社区生态的沟通平台和媒介，使社区成为非常重要的与消费者沟通的渠道，社群营销也将会有更大的突破；
- 未来在社区生态内也将产生更多的场景，需要在不同的社区场景上为消费者提供更适合的沟通与连接，帮助商业机构和品牌成为社区生态的重要组成部分；
- 品牌将有更大的发挥空间，将品牌的文化和理念以更深入社区和社群的方式与消费者进行沟通，并且推动社区和谐健康的发展。

8. 未来的健康

新冠肺炎疫情再次将公众的目光投向了医疗行业，同时将医疗行业推向了传统的行业边界之外，加深了与其他行业的交流。同时，在全面的政策支持下，国家推出“健康中国”战略，鼓励为实现全民健康而努力。在国家政策的扶持下，各产业也开始合作，提供全系统、全场景的健康服务。

我们的提问：在未来，我们能否更轻松管理自己以及家人在不同人生阶段的健康状况?

畅想未来健康的图景小故事

谁说他们只是AI（人工智能）？

周日下午，在一个室内羽毛球场。

卡罗尔微微弯腰，握紧球拍，竖起她原本温柔的眉毛，眼睛警觉地盯着对面那个摆起发球姿势的年轻人。看似不小心倾斜的手腕把球推到了球网上空，但是球太高了！注意到这一“疏忽”，她立刻向球扑去。只见她往后退了一步，又猛地跃起，把球狠狠地砸了回去。一记漂亮的杀球，把男孩打了个措手不及。对面的男孩咧嘴笑了笑。他没有像卡罗尔预想的那样猝不及防，而是径直冲到网前，一如既往毫不费力地，用有如教科书式的回击把球打进了她的网前。

由于太远没能接住球，卡罗尔对着记分牌摇了摇头，略显烦恼，她拿起球，准备再次发球。

几轮下来，卡罗尔已经是大汗淋漓，比赛终于结束了。与气喘吁吁、满头大汗的卡罗尔相反，那个镇静自若的年轻陪练，建议她休息一天，她点点头表示同意。转眼间，体育场、球场、陪练伙伴都淡淡隐去，她所处的是一间明亮的空房间。

这样的训练方式，成为卡罗尔每周周末惯常的活动已经有些时候了。这种虚拟现实模拟羽毛球课由一位名叫小风的个人健康经理主持——这个人工智能程序已经陪伴了她近10年了。随后，通过每周总结卡罗尔向小风了解了她这周的表现："和过去一个月的记录相比，你显然进步了不少……。"卡罗尔静静地听着最新的数据反馈，从神经反射间隔到心率、卡路里燃烧和体脂率的情况——下降了约3%。午后阳光灿烂温暖，卡罗尔一边听着数据，一边慢慢向家中走去。

但最后的一项数据引起了她的关注。卡罗尔已经松了一口气的眉头又蹙在了一起。"喂，小风，现在进度会不会太慢了？我能做些什么来让进度快一点吗？"感觉到她有点激动，小风用温柔的男声回应："别担心，卡罗尔，你做得很好，现在你要做的就是试着享受这一刻"。

"真的吗？什么都不用做吗？"她听起来有些难以置信。

"当然。你知道我最近注意到什么吗？你只是对我为你制订的饮食和健身计划太过焦虑了——我很想补充一句，你已经做得很完美了！放松下来、慢一点、适度停停对你是最好的。当然，我跟你一样希望你健康美丽。但是，别忘了偶尔对自己微笑一下，拍拍自己的胸口，肯定现在的自己，好吗？”

卡罗尔长长地舒了口气。当她回到三楼的公寓时，她终于舒展了眉头。在那个阳光明媚的下午，她打开了柔和的爵士乐，双颊重新挂上了温柔的微笑。

这微笑，一整天都不肯散去。

未来健康趋势关键词

我们相信未来会出现：

智能健康管理伴一生

全面设计的医疗保健行业，涵盖所有生命阶段

- 全方位的大健康观贯穿整个生命周期，不同阶段都有不同层面的防控和干预；
- 健康的多元定义：身、心、外观、生活方式、家庭与社群关系；
- 综合支持体系和个性化方案，搭载贴心服务；
- 科技主导的更体系化的个人健康管理：监测、预防、分诊、后服务等。

科技如何赋能未来?

“预防为主，治疗为辅”将成为未来医疗保健的主要模式，健康管理、精确检测、治疗和康复将确保整体公共健康。同时，国家医保与商业医疗保险的普及，将有望减轻个人在医疗方面的负担。

未来可穿戴设备、远程医疗、双向音视频远程、慢性病监测、区块链医学等高科技将在医学领域大范围应用。人工智能、“物联网+”等新技术将为大健康产业带来变革，将大大提升诊断治疗的智能化的水平。此外，未来将通过精准的检测、治疗、康养来实现个性化、专业化的全生命周期健康的照顾管理系统。精确的个性化专业医疗管理将不再仅仅是梦想。

杏树林创始人及CEO/张遇升

未来30年我们将面对人口急剧老化问题，将有超过一半的人口是60岁以上老人。整个健康医疗行业亟待解决的是一切和变老有关的需求。

一个更健康的自我会给你带来什么样的可能性？

关于未来健康的乐观预期和带有争议性的评论

在未来，人们将获得哪些利益点？

更全面的健康	帮助人们获得除身体健康外的心理健康，以及更健康的生活方式
更受关注和关爱	更多机构参与提供健康服务，给予生活上的贴心照顾
更高效的医疗保健	远程诊疗技术，照护资源有效分配
更易防控疾病风险	实时、快速、准确地监测自己或家人的健康状况
更精准的解决方案	效率分诊，科学分析，精准判断，提供最佳解决方案
医疗资源更平衡	医疗分级、共享电子病历、共享医疗体系将极大改善高低线城市之间医疗资源的供需矛盾
更安心	对健康更有掌控，对未来的健康有更好的阶段性规划

同时，我们也会担忧：

尽管数字化医疗体系无疑优化了个人和集体健康管理，但它仍未能解决迫在眉睫的难题，如缺乏体育锻炼导致的肥胖、过度使用屏幕导致的视力下降、独居和社会边缘化导致的孤独感。另外，是否还会出现某些新的疾病或者身体机能的退化呢？

医疗改革将给我们带来哪些新的挑战？我们如何才能更好地应对新的疾病暴发？

健康监测科技的普及让我们时刻掌握自己的身体状况，但是否会让人们对于自己身体的健康的变化过度反应（尤其是老人和孩子），造成过度焦虑？

医学的发展会缩短不同年龄阶段的人在外貌和健康状况上的差异，如此，是否会大大改变人们之间互动的方式？

知乎上网友的脑洞提问：

在可预见的未来，有哪些疾病可能被消灭？

未来医学可以根治近视吗？

现代人都变得有头部前倾的倾向了吗？应如何预防？

全球老龄化后，未来的公共医疗会有怎样的变化？

来自知乎上专家的提问：

林翠芬（Ann Lim）
蔚迈中国，首席客户官
知乎 ID：Hedonistann

我相信：我们往往容易低估“现在”对“未来”的影响——即，我们今天面临的挑战将成为寻找未来解决方案的原生力量。我们不断追求更好的过程，终将使我们在未来获得一种“超人”的状态。

- 未来，精神压力可以被完全消除吗？
- 身体疲劳是否能充分被预防？
- 80%以上的医疗健康服务是否将会以虚拟方式被提供？
- 未来的手术仍然需要（人类）医生来操作吗？
- 除了透过饮食、运动和手术，我们是否有其他方式可以改变我们的身体和外观？

陈毅（Echo Chen）
爱乐甜（健康零卡糖品牌），品牌总监
知乎 ID：门里一条虫

我相信：自由、平权、个性。

- 长命百岁变成标配，人们还想要什么？
- 以后会不会研发出真正有效不伤身体的减肥药？
- 有没有被动式方案让人躺赢健康人生？

- 以后会不会有更多超越现有身体素质的运动极限被开发或探索出来？
- 好多好多代同堂真的是件幸福的事情吗？

未来的商业和营销机遇：

商业启示

- 医疗保健行业已成为近年来的焦点：各产业均可以健康为突破口，为自身的发展寻找新的增长点。健康产业已经成为风口，随着人们生活水平的不断提高，对健康的需求也会越来越多，健康将会成为更多产品或服务必不可少的价值点；
- 全方位监测：开发适合在家庭、办公室、公共场所等场景下可以使用的健康管理设备。例如，可以与家具、办公设备或公共设施相结合，实时、快速、准确地监测自己、家人或员工的健康状况，并可实时给出解决方案。

营销启示

- 所有产业的营销都可以站在健康营销的风口：营销已经破圈，它不再是医药企业的专属，其他品类的品牌可以将健康这一概念，运用到品牌的各种市场营销活动中；
- 品牌完全融于人们的健康生活方式中，并成为健康生活方式的倡导者，推动社会健康事业的发展；

- 作为营销机构和平台，可以努力促进产业融合，帮助各个产业的品牌整合服务与模式，为消费者打造整体健康生活方式与服务模式；
- 挖掘消费者对健康的不同需求与身体状况，精准地匹配营销内容以及适合的解决方案，如不同的健康产品与运动方式的组合。

9. 未来的社交

随着娱乐和工作领域的扩展，个人社交网络正逐渐超越其传统的界限。除此之外，社交媒体平台在扩展和维持现有的线上+线下社交圈方面，发挥着关键的、越来越重要的基础性作用，更不用说帮我们保持多重身份了。未来的我们须在不同的背景和需求下与对不同的自我进行灵活切换。

我们的提问：在未来，更复杂的社交关系和多元身份会如何拓宽我们生命的宽度？

畅想未来社交的图景小故事

独立群居：在维度之间游历

大山总认为自己是个无可救药的怀旧的人，向往过去的日子所带来的切实的温暖。如果让他在现在和过去之间做出选择，他会毫不犹豫地离开现在的城市环境，回到那个更简单、更人性化的过去。

然而，尽管大山每天都被冰冷的高科技淹没，他还是偶然发现有这么一些技术，让自己感觉更舒心自在。大山没有与都市的躁动一起随波逐流，也没有大隐隐于市，泯然众人。大多数时候，他宁愿关掉闹钟，睡个回笼觉，亲手做一顿丰盛的早午餐，戴上他的黑框眼镜，在舒适的沙发上读读书。

有时，被朋友戏称为“保守派”的大山会进入“冬眠”，取而代之的是“复古派”大山。

作为怀旧协会的创始成员，大山有幸租用了一个完整的虚拟星球，来建造怀旧总部。在这个地球大小的虚拟星球上，没有春天的沙尘暴和冬天的雾霾，也没有腐烂的垃圾填埋场和漂浮的塑料。大山欢迎各种各样的游客——人类和人工智能——来到他精心打理、一尘不染的梦想世界。如果天气好的话，他会穿上21世纪初的衣服，跳上一辆敞篷车，接上茜茜——他虚拟的女友（她“住在”离他最喜欢的房子只有几个街区远的地方），然后一起度过一个“亲密周末”。

有时，他们会随性在某家唱片店停留，随意挑选一张唱片，在昏暗的橙色灯光下静静地聆听一整个下午；如果愿意，他们也会去当地的跳蚤市场，大山特别喜欢那儿的一个相熟的皮具老板——两人每次见面，都会聊上几个小时，讨论到现在几乎失传的制鞋或手袋的传统工艺，以及它们背后独特而丰富的历史。

随着他的星球吸引了更多的来访者，这个怀旧协会的会员人数也不断地增加，许多人都希望他们能找个时间真正地线下聚一聚。

经过了一个月的谋划和联络，线下见面的活动终于得以落地。本周末，怀旧协会在许多城市都租用了场地举办怀旧主题聚会。大山希望这些聚会能提高协会的社会影响力，最终让网友们得以见面，而不是让大家总是相隔于屏幕、相忘于江湖。

在为期两天的活动结束后，越来越多的访客来到了大山的怀旧星球，人数远远超出他的预期。许多人在短暂体验了怀旧生活的VR世界之后，纷纷注册了会员，同时提供了大量的反馈意见。大山认为这些反馈大大有利于即将到来的怀旧星球的系统升级。

随着时间的推移，大山成了一个怀旧界的名人，这一切看起来，与他淡泊名利的初衷渐行渐远。除此之外，他最新的时尚作品将怀旧的设计工艺和当代极简主义融为一体，变得像他那个孤独、拥挤，但不乏温馨的数字星球一样受到欢迎。

未来社交趋势关键词

我们相信未来会出现：

平行世界中的多重自我

不同空间的不同身份

随着职业需求的迅速多样化，业余爱好将成为扩大现有社交圈的主要推动力。同时，“斜杠青年”[1]的大量出现，也会增加他们的多重身份。此外，科技也帮助我们打破地域文化的界限，深度维护好与他人的关系。其中一个例子就是斜杠运动（Alboher，2012），它在通过广泛的技术支持的个人网络将传统工作和休闲领域融合在一起的基础上，

1 “斜杠青年”，指代的是在同一时间段内拥有超过一种职业身份的人。它在这个时代被概念化地提出，并成为一个社会现象被人们越来越多地谈论。甚至有人说，我们的社会已经进入了“斜杠时代”。

还改变了社会的意义，使个人生活日益多元化。

我们可以进一步设想，甚至我们的社会身份或民族特性也可以虚拟化（如虚拟国籍），为我们的生活带来无限可能。

科技如何赋能未来？

随着碎片化生活的加剧，我们每个人都需要多元的生活、多重的身份来表达自我，由此催生了一个个虚拟的平行世界，2021年Facebook推出的Horizon社交VR平台便是一种尝试，这一平台不再局限于游戏里的线上社交。

在未来5—7年内，我们可能会看到大规模在线数字平行世界的兴起，这将在质量上超越之前的技术和平台。例如在线论坛和MMORPG（大规模多人在线角色扮演游戏）中的数字社交世界，带来更有意义的第二人生。此外，虚拟身份甚至可以整合到真实身份识别系统中，为我们的身份识别开辟了未知的领域。

洞察及教育创新专家/Candy Yang

未来线上将反哺线下的生活，比如带来新的友谊和工作机会。也许我们可以通过线上更有效地安排个性化的生活，把时间更多花在更有兴趣和价值的事情上。

在虚拟世界承诺提供的看似取之不尽、用之不竭的身份中，你最渴望的是什么，你希望在这些身份下过什么样的生活？

关于未来社交的乐观预期和带有争议性的评论

在未来，人们将获得哪些利益点？

拓宽视野	地域文化的界限被打破
助力事业发展	社交圈的拓展，带来更多的人脉资源，带动事业的发展
丰富人生体验	虚拟化身份（甚至虚拟国籍），使人们能够从不同的角度体验原本无法理解的生活
更易维护关系	更多渠道和平台帮助人们维护不同社群的关系
提高社交能力	社交机会的增多，帮助人们提升社交能力
找到归属感	更容易找到志同道合的同伴和社群

同时，我们也会担忧：

长时期在虚拟世界中与他人交流，而缺乏与现实社会接触，是否会导致一些人对线下现实产生不真实的期望，造成某些心理或精神问题的出现？

社群或圈子中意见的同质化和两极分化可能会成为一个重要问题，而不同的声音或意见更难有发声的机会，是否会使“沉默的螺旋”*现象普遍发生？

随着社交圈子的愈加细分化，同时进入某个圈子的门槛可能也变得更高。是否会花费我们更多时间打理自己在不同社交圈层的“人设”而形成负担，引发焦虑，危害我们的幸福？

* “沉默的螺旋”（The Spiral Of Silence）最早见于诺埃勒-诺依曼（Noelle-Neumann）1974年在《传播学：沉默的螺旋刊》上发表的一篇论文，1980年以德文出版的《沉默的螺旋：舆论——我们的社会皮肤》一书，对这个理论进行了全面的概括。沉默的螺旋来源于这样一个事实：1965年德国阿兰斯（Allensbach）研究所对即将到来的德国大选进行了研究。在研究过程中，两个政党即基督教民主党和社会民主党在竞选中处于并驾齐驱的状况，第一次估计的结果出来，两党均有获胜的机会。然而6个月后，即在大选前的2个月，基督教民主党与社会民主党获胜的可能性是4 ：1，对基督教民主党在政治上的胜利期望升高有很大的帮助。在大选前的最后两周，基督教民主党赢得了4%的选票，社会民主党失去了5%的选票。在1965年的大选中，基督教民主党以领先9%的优势赢得了大选。这一年大选带来的困惑和对它的解释逐渐发展成为沉默的螺旋的概念。沉默的螺旋概念基本描述了这样一个现象：人们在表达自己想法和观点的时候，如果看到自己赞同的观点，并且受到广泛欢迎，就会积极参与进来，这类观点越发大胆地发表和扩散；而发觉某一观点无人或很少有人理会（有时会有群起而攻之的遭遇），即使自己赞同它，也会保持沉默。意见一方的沉默造成另一方意见的增势，如此循环往复，便形成一方的声音越来越强大，另一方越来越沉默下去的螺旋发展过程。

知乎上网友的脑洞提问：

未来的社交网络是什么样子的？现有的社交模式靠谱吗？

社恐症在虚拟社交中，可以被治愈吗？

未来你想拥有哪些虚拟身份？

如果你可以选择拥有虚拟国籍，你幻想加入怎样的虚拟国度？

来自知乎上专家的提问：

梁笑（Sean Liang）
Soul App 公关总监
知乎 ID：Soul App

我相信：无论未来科技如何发展，人都应是目的而不是手段。

- 人类还会有主动去认识新朋友的需求吗？
- 线下还会是人们进行社交的主要场合吗？
- 我们能跟人工智能交朋友吗？
- 会有科技帮人类传递无法用语言表达的心意吗？
- 人的心灵意识可以被数据化吗？

劳博

广告门 CEO，专注于品牌、传播行业、策略及创意的超级融合，希望搭建起一座超级桥梁。

知乎 ID：劳博

我相信：交流使人进步

- 互联网解决了线上交流的可能，人们会因此失去线下交流的欲望吗？
- 最便捷的社交方式会是什么？是寻求见面，还是随时随地的线上交流？
- 线上专业交流，更多通过聊天，还是专业发问？
- 最难交流的问题是什么？人类的交流，在进步还是退步？

未来的商业和营销机遇：

商业启示

- 在开发平台或产品时，除为了考虑社交属性而增加社交功能之外，给消费者提供更切实的社交利益点；
- 除了工具的开发，例如帮助来自不同地域、不同文化背景的人与人之间的沟通的语音识别和翻译工具，更多的机遇在于场景与价值；
- 更细分、更垂直的社交工具和平台，让更多的人可以找到志同道合的伙伴和社群。

营销启示

- 品牌更多地参与到社交话题的创建中，引导和推动社会积极价值观的建立和传播；
- 未来，更多平台将“变身”社交平台，为品牌提供更多的深度沟通机遇。这需要清晰理解不同的、新兴的社交平台的角色和价值，进行更细致的社交营销矩阵设计；
- 为品牌寻找更细分精确的社交平台和社群，更精准地与目标受众沟通；尤其是对于多元身份的消费者，需要识别在不同社群与场景下的需求差异，提升沟通的有效性。

10. 未来的数据资产

随着数字领域越来越成为我们生活中不可或缺的一部分，公众对其每天产生的惊人数量数据的去向的认识也会逐渐成为一个重要的议题。

现今，我们的数据安全意识已经在逐步加强，对数据隐私的关切度也在提升。然而，立法者在法律上承认个人数据是个人财产方面进展缓慢，我们很难明确知晓个人数据在哪存储，被谁使用，如何使用，更难掌控自己的个人数据。数据泄露、盗用或非法使用仍然屡见不鲜。

我们的提问：我们的数据将成为带来价值的资产，还是冗余的负累？

畅想未来数据的图景小故事

赚了翻倍，这样就可以了？

当王小利检查他长期关闭提醒的数据库账户时，不由得吃了一惊。他忍不住目瞪口呆地看着眼前的东西。事实证明，在最近这一次非自愿遗忘事件中，他发现自己消费数据的授权使用价格几乎翻了一倍，也就是说，如果有企业或者商家想得到他这部分数据并向他推销些什么的话，必须得加价了。但显然，他还未因为开放数据获得收益。

仔细想想，王小利意识到他可能有点反应过度了。确实，在过去的一年里，这位刚订婚的男士对婚礼筹备的工作相当认真。他购买了很多东西：家具家电、家居用品、西装婚纱、对戒项链等。从寻找家电和家具的经济套餐到策划实际活动，他会花数小时在网上发表评论，使用了各种比较工具，像一个完美主义者那样时不时地讨价还价。最后，当待办事项清单上的所有项目最终确定后，他像往常一样从电子商务平台上获得了一份完整的数据日志。这些数据在经过网站和电商搜集打包后，发送给数据银行进行保存和管理。银行则通过AI和大数据分析，对这部分数据进行识别和精确归类，并打上了“婚礼筹备”的标签。

他几乎忘记了一切——直到刚才。

在他没有察觉的情况下，他惯常使用的人工智能助理已经帮他整理好了数据，将每个项目——家具成本效益、该地区最佳婚礼场地等——归档在相关标题下。市场上已经有很成熟的个人数据的竞价购买机制，这一机制目的就是让供求关系来决定数据资产的价格。

在求购数据的企业名单中，王小利看到了有知名酒店、航空公司、旅行社、婚纱摄影、花店等他即将为婚礼所花销的项目。另外，还有月子中心、早教机构和售楼中心，似乎都非常渴望为他规划未来。

“看来我还挺受欢迎。”，他用手指敲打着桌面，咧嘴笑了，忽然有种众星捧月的满足感。笑到一半的时候，突然出现了一个通知，提示赤裸裸地告诉他一个新的竞购者愿意花费10%的溢价来购买他的健康数据。他很感兴趣，打开了消息。

原来是一家运动康复机构，正在研发一种治疗过度劳累导致的突发性心力衰竭的药物，为此而求购爱好运动的人士的手环数据。而小利正好是这个药物的目标人群，平时也会通过运动手环将身体各项数据同步到数据中心。

在对该机构做了简单的研究之后，他决定免费与该研究所分享所有的健康数据文件。因为王小利坚信，除了商业价值之外，个人数据还应为共同创造一个更美好的未来做出贡献。

整整一个下午，小利都沉浸在喜悦之中。

未来数据趋势关键词

我们相信未来会出现：

数据资产化

个人数据成为所有权受法律保护的资产

随着数字技术的进步，个人数据将成为个人资产。因此，它可以存放在数据库中，并且只能由第三方通过所有者授权使用——这除了使个人数据更安全之外，还需要新的方法来有效利用数字资产，从而发展出更多的用途和使用场景。

科技如何赋能未来?

未来，数据将发挥更大的作用，也会衍生出越来越多的用途（如售卖、交易等）。随着围绕个人数据的所有权结构更加明确，个人数据演变成一种货币或一种类似可以其他人交易或出售的商品，也许只是时间问题。因此，建立健全的数据管理机制是非常紧迫的。基于区块链技术的数据库将在保护我们数字资产组合的未来安全方面发挥至关重要的作用。

同时，数据安全需求的不断增长将催生新的行业和商机，比如阻止数据泄露的AI数据安全顾问、基于数据泄露风险的个人保险、信号收集屏蔽的隔离度假区等。

未来将完善数据共享和使用机制，在法律监管下，政府、企业、消费者达成多方共识，在有效利用数据的同时，保证个人的权益，可能形成私人数据档案管理。

5G技术专家/芮斌

5G的速度更快，能带来更大的数据量，因此对数据的安全也提出了更高的挑战。同时，数据将成为未来的个人资产，并以技术加密的方式进行开放和分享。

在所有你的个人数据中，你觉得哪些是最为珍贵且不可交易的？

关于未来数据的乐观预期和带有争议性的评论

在未来，人们将获得哪些利益点？

更安全	当数据成为资产，其安全性会进一步提升
更多隐私保护	个人都能够将自己的数据存入数据银行，由本人授权才能使用
更多的财富和应用价值	数据成为个人资产的一部分，并且可以变现或交易
获取更定制化的产品或服务	可以授权数据进行使用和分析，获得更具针对性的产品和服务
对自己的数据更有掌控感	获得数据所有权，并拥有完整的法律保护
更好的自我分析和规划	人工智能帮助审查和分析个人数据，以制订更好的计划

同时，我们也会担忧：

新一代通信技术带来的信息量爆炸是否会加剧数字领域的

现有困境，并不可逆转地使我们的日常生活复杂化，以至于可能在某个时候导致某些无法克服的数据可管理性障碍？

私人数据所有权的合法化是否会给现有的网络犯罪（如盗版、篡改或欺诈）提供更丰富和可操作的理由？

知乎上网友的脑洞提问：

在未来的大数据时代，我们学习、生活和工作将会发生哪些有趣的变化？

未来，我们如何避免被困在系统里？

数据能怎样更好地帮我们回顾过去？或启发未来的路？

使用了我们个人数据，再把广告投放给我们的商业模式，未来会如何破局？

把一个人大脑里所有数据都存储上传，能让人脱离肉体永生吗？

来自知乎上专家的提问：

张谦（Jason Zhang）

小米集团，总监

知乎 ID：digication

我相信：人类或将进化为全新物种，活动半径为全宇宙。

- 未来的记忆数据可以集合在芯片放进大脑里吗？
- 如果未来一切都是数据化的，这个世界还是真实的吗？
- 如果未来的连接不再依靠互联网会依靠什么？
- 如果可随意查到任何人一生的数据会发生什么？

郭琳（Lisa Guo）
群邑中国程序化及平台服务董事总经理
知乎 ID：Lisa

我相信：未来的模样不可预测。毫无疑问，科技的发展会让生活、工作、沟通更加便捷。但无论科技如何发展，人类社会特有的信任、共情、责任感，都不可被磨灭。我们需要共创一个以“人文关怀”为底色的数字化未来。

- 在未来，数据是否会有明确归属权，并明确被划分为公共数据或私人数据？
- 在未来，数据可否变成一种资产被赠与或被继承？
- 在未来，人们是否会迎来数据过剩的时代，身处大量无法处理的数据而无法自拔？
- 在未来，是否会出现专门的“数据垃圾清理工”？

张洪雷
虎嗅，图书编辑
知乎 ID：孤独图书会

我相信：人类的未来会越来越好，直到奇点发声。

- 被数据和算法操控的世界，普通人还有没有未来？
- 大数据时代，如何保护我们的隐私？

未来的商业和营销机遇：

商业启示

- 未来可能出现“数据资产银行”，为个人保存数据资产；
- 未来也可能出现“数据交易所”，催生出更多的数据交易模式与产品，例如获得消费者数据的新模式；
- 针对不同的数据维度为消费者提供定制化的服务。

营销启示

- 未来可能会出现新的沟通方式，例如对公开数据以及资产化数据的使用会发展出不同的信息匹配或交易模式；
- 未来需要更好地针对个人数据，提供更多的价值，以激励数据在营销领域的良性使用；
- 未来会需要与不同类型的数据平台进行深度合作，基于用户授权的数据进行使用和分析，匹配和组合更具针对性的品牌、产品和服务；

- 品牌在个人数据的使用或管理上要起表率作用（如苹果IOS14系统会主动询问是否同意App访问同一网络中的其他设备，来限制第三方应用追踪或使用个人信息）。

结语

我们通往未来的旅程终于要落下帷幕。

在一个变革无处不在、创新成为日常流行语的时代，我们总是发现自己不断地站在十字路口，遥望未来，并发表着对于未来的态度与期望。

透过这本书，我们试图阐明对可预见的未来的观点。我们希望，随着好奇心的觉醒，此刻，你已经在脑海中初步勾勒出关于未来的草图——也许还会有更多的问题需要被提出和思考。

未来是更加积极而美好的。当科学技术、文化和经济的发展使我们进一步从日常生活中解放出来，在个人和社会层面发挥我们的各种潜力时，相较于过去时代，现在我们更像是自己人生故事的编剧、导演和演员。我们所需要的只是勇敢地挑战今天摆在我们面前的一切，大胆地对明天产生好奇和想象。

我们相信，由于技术民主化和定制化的持续发展趋势，参与塑造未来不再是美好的白日梦。相反，技术推动者与其创造者之间日益增强的共生关系，预示着不久的将来，我们每个人都可以为自己选择或设计向往的生活——无论是从过去的不满中重新开始，还是延续引以为豪的过往。

我们希望未来的你在回首今朝时，会对现在所做的选择给予积极的肯定，并且认识到此刻在你脑海中萌动的好奇有多珍贵。

欢迎你打开知乎，搜索“关于未来的提问”或“提问未来”，进入“我们关于未来的提问”讨论专区，大胆提出你的问题，并与网友们分享你的答案。

关于未来的提问

OUR QUESTIONS TO THE FUTURE

Edited by
Linna Zhao

上海社会科学院出版社
SHANGHAI ACADEMY OF SOCIAL SCIENCES PRESS

关 于 未 来 的 提 问

· Our Questions to the Future

知乎 × Wavemaker

Project Team

Linna Zhao
Project Initiator, Editor of this book
Thought Leadership, Wavemaker

Linna leads the Thought Leadership Sector in Wavemaker China, focusing on transforming research and practice into knowledge to be shared in our industry. Her team has released content with different studies like “UNSEEN” documentary series, “Seniors in China, the Hidden Value” report series, “Digital Children in China” report, “Quality of Life in China Whitepaper”, “Generation Z in China” report, etc.

Robbie Zhang
Project Co-initiator
General Manager of Commercial Marketing Department, Zhihu

Robbie Zhang leads a team at Zhihu business strategy and development sector, focusing on Zhihu’s commercial value mining, brand building, marketing solutions for commercial revenue, investment promotion & IP projects, etc.

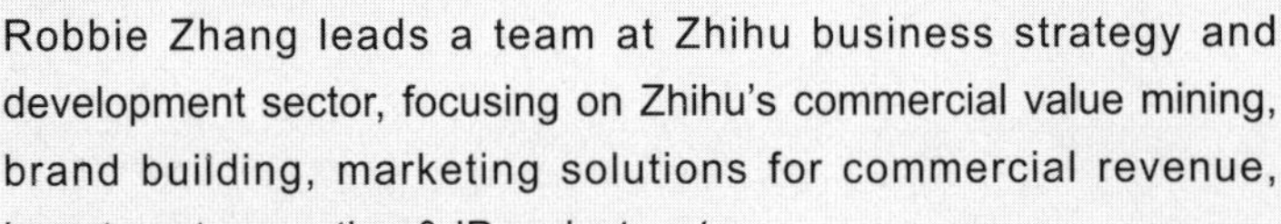

In 2020, the “Zhihu Social Innovation Lab” was launched to promote Zhihu’s exploration in the fields of innovative public welfare and social innovation.

Qiwen Cui
Project Co-initiator
Content Officer, BottleDream

Qiwen Cui is the content officer of BottleDream, a social innovation community, focusing on long-term public issues such as climate change, technology for good, and engaging in public communication. Since the pandemic in 2020, she participated in many social collaborations. Piror to that, she was a tech reporter at QDaily covering technologies and social good in Silicon Valley and Beijing.

Foreword

When it comes to the future, perhaps we do care.

After all, why not? We might all be familiar with having to pick a side on upcoming major life events, such as quitting or switching jobs, where to finally settle down, marriage and children — or even the purpose of life. It is almost as though caring about the future is something to be taken for granted. Whether thinking or not, the future will come as promised, and we will continue to move forward.

However, instead of waiting for the future to happen quietly and passively accept the arrival of the future, why not become more active to enter the future more fearlessly and with a better sense of control?

Perhaps that is why when talking about the future, a consistent principle seems to be absent. One can easily imagine elucidating on one's positions on child-raring, marriage, career — but when it comes to the future, do you know where you stand?

In all fairness, it appears that we carry with us a grey lens when looking at the future. The most popular postwar cinema on future often plunges one down a rabbit hole that resembles not much

else than a screaming ride of dystopic rollercoaster, with household topics ranging from alien invasion (*Alien*), virus outbreak (*Pandemic*), extreme situations (Wandering Earth), superhuman (any one of those marvel movies), and the fan favorite — humans being dethroned and replaced by robots (The Matrix). It seems that the film and television works about the future have reached a "consensus" to a certain extent, that is, starting with the tone of pessimism, and finally closing with adhering to the positive values to draw a period of hope.

If you zoom in to see the Chinese culture that respects diligence and pragmatism, there are four words come to my mind: 远虑 (yuan—distant + lv—concern, *prepared for danger in times of peace*, *take precautions*, and *worry about the world prior to anything*), 久长 (jiu—persistent + chang—long, "*next life*", "*500 years later*", "*centenary, millennium*, *long live*"), 非吾 (fei—not + wu—me, our control over the future seems to be based on the outside, such as luck, Feng Shui and destiny), and 愿能 (yuan—wish + neng—capable, we believe in proactive initiative, for example, *man can conquer nature*, and *there will be times when wind and waves break through*). Our culture focuses more on the macro perspective.

To gain more insights on public perspectives vis-à-vis the future, Wavemaker China and Zhihu launched a performance art project at this year's Maker Faire Shanghai — one of the largest global maker conventions. We gathered questions to the future from the event's dynamic and curious makers, together created a hundred-meter long *Curious Route* using traditional Chinese calligraphy, and invited participants to cocreate a collage exhibition about the future.

Between children and adults, we see very recognizable differences.

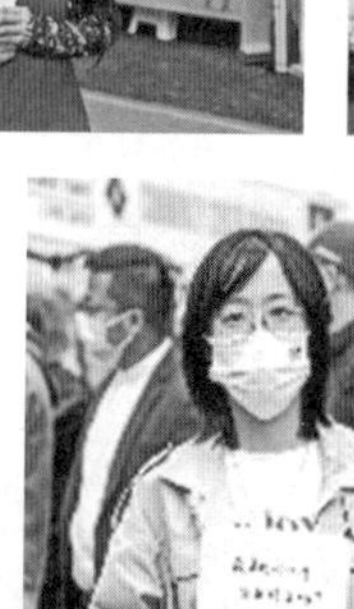

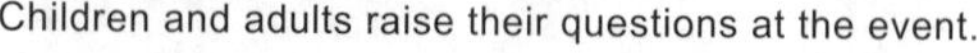

Children and adults raise their questions at the event.

The one-hundred-meter *Curious Route*, with children and adults questions to the future written on it

Collage exhibition on the theme of *future hopes*.

For starters, when relating to the future, children tend to use *I*, whereas adults favor positioning themselves on a higher perspective, using terms such as *humanity, society, people*, etc. On the other hand, children's imagination towards the future are more optimistic and less bound by material circumstance; by contrast, adults often approach the topic with sober calculation, and are more likely to dwell on the bigger questions of the day, such as *will technological progress eliminate the weakness in human nature?, when will be the world become more tolerant?, when will ideals be not just pipedreams?, will connections between family members and friends be weaker in the future?*, and so on.

Put side by side,

Children tend to be more ...	**Adults tend to be more ...**
Imaginative	Paradoxical
Micro	Macro
Material	Abstract
Emotional	Rational
Fun	Reasonable
Righteous	Orderly

What is more curious is that be it adults or children, their questions are frequently framed as a yes-or-no question, as if by formatting as such, a simple, unambiguous answer exists somewhere, waiting patiently to be discovered. (e.g., *will average human life expectancy reach 100 years? Will national boundaries become a thing of the past? Will further globalization bring progress or regression? Will technology further accentuate existing differences between people and countries? Will pollution be solved in the future?*)

Maybe we really need to think about the future in more methodical ways.

How then, can it be done?

The most vital step, is to ask.

According to Harvard developmental psychologist Paul Harris, between the age of 2 and 5, a child asks an average of 40,000 questions. But as we age, the questions we raise steadily decrease — as adults, we don't seem to be that fond of questions at all.

Knowing this, we should keep in mind to never regard a question as something to be taken-for-granted, a quotidian routine is simple or even *natural.* Despite the fact that the capability to ask is within each of us by birth, the motivation to ask decreases as we age. As we become entangled in more routines and responsibilities in a familiar world, we increasingly favor answers that are direct and simple, whereas thinking — an endeavor that consumes enormous amount of energy — steadily gets sidelined in the name of efficiency.

This is why we partnered with Zhihu in launching our social innovation project *Questions to the Future*.

Because Zhihu believes: with each answer, there awaits answers.

We believe: with curiosity, there will be action.

Questioning is, after all, a craft, and there are methods and systems to better performing it. The four most important tools are *What, How, Why,* and *What if.* These innocuous looking words are the wellspring behind all our explorations and experimentations.

What and *How* are used to explore and state facts, *Why* is used for step-by-step analysis, *What if* is used to formulate hypotheses. The exploration, verification, and planning we are about to engage in will come back to *What, How,* and *Why*.

Depending on your proposition and goals, the same structures scan be extended to ask a wide variety of questions. In business, we

often customize specific frameworks for different propositions and objectives, which consists of different methodologies, frameworks, brainstorming and co-construction methods, etc., all of which need to be designed for specific situation.

Here I'm simply sharing a straightforward logic. To support each step in delving deeper into questioning, the four structures are most crucial.

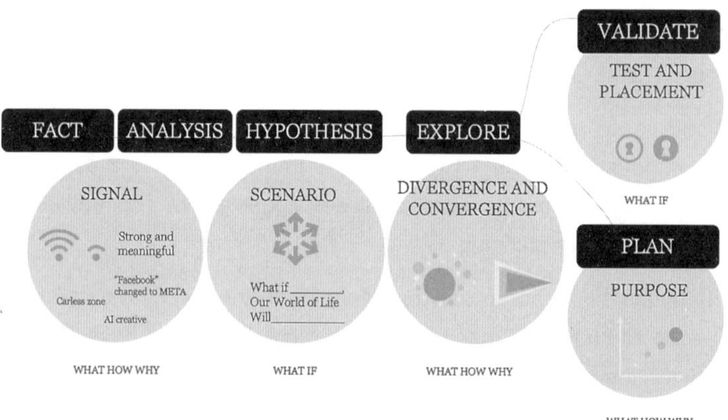

The basic logical structure for thinking about the future

Knowing the importance of questioning and its structure is not enough — don't forget to set a timer. If you lose a sense of scale, future becomes too distant.

Try to imagine the future in 50 years, do you see a clear picture? What about 30 years, 20, 10? They are all likely to be murky. But what if its one year, do you feel more in control?

Let's open up the scale and take a look. 1 year, it appears, is *the* tipping point for future certainty, as it is much harder for people to plan more than one year ahead. For instance, prior to the epidemic,

when it comes to purchasing long-term products such as overseas travel product, regardless of how low the prices reached, most purchases were clustered within the one-year timeframe, for there is much less certainty about what will happen beyond the mark.

As a result, we need to increase certainty when approaching future planning — future as in a time that is more than one year away, with limited amount of immediately controllable certainty.

Then how long a timeline, when thinking about the future, is more meaningful?

There is no one answer. If the goal is to direct concrete actions, we suggest to define 1 to 2 years as immediate, 3 to 5 as short-term, and 10 years as deadline to set bigger goals. This applies to corporate future planning as well.

Naturally, this is not to say that planning further is without meaning (as we all know that many forward-looking enterprises have already defined their horizon as 30 or 50 years in the future), it is simply that a 1 to 10-year timeline is more likely to direct concrete action if we

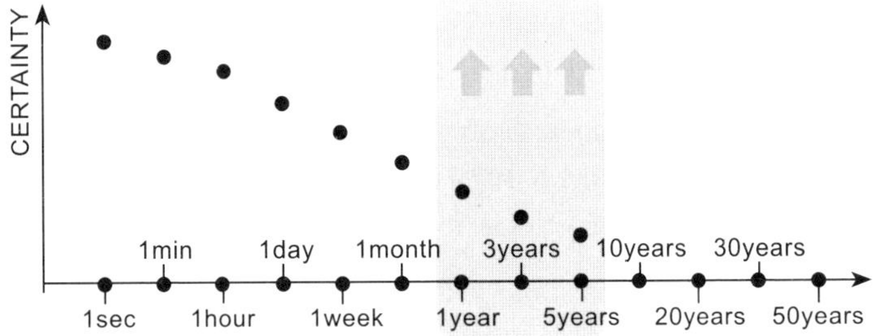

Certainty vis-à-vis timeline

are focusing on short-to-mid-term planning.

In this book, we set the timer at one decade.

The ten-year frame here, we want to remind the reader, is a hypothetical setting for thought experiment, not for prediction of any sort. Who would have thought AI — born in postwar computer labs in the 1950s, only become truly functional today, or how the ongoing pandemic fast-forwarded smart city development?

Under the framework of a decade, we illustrate the future through ten "real-life" scenarios:

- WHAT: What will become the new mainstream?
- HOW: How does technology unlock the future?
- WHY: Why are we solving the questions that we are solving?

We hope that by following this model, you can be inspired to think more of *What if* questions. As such, please understand this book is by no means exclusively dedicated to methodology. What we wish to achieve is by encouraging raising questions, more people will be inspired to engage the future intellectually.

Naturally, there are three other equally crucial steps after raising the question. They are:

First. Definition — to define your own future value.

From *what can I do* to *what do I need to do, to what must I do*, set up a layer-by-layer structure to help you define your life mission, and transform it into specific goals, plans and actions.

Mr. YUAN Longping (known as the Father of Hybrid Rice in China), whom I respect very much, had very clear personal missions. What he did was something he thought *must* be done, which was also his

life's mission and what he actually did.

The most valuable global brands know how to define their own future brand value as well. Looking at the top three brands on the BrandZ brand value global ranking list — Amazon, Apple, and Microsoft, the actions they commit are all based on their core missions and beliefs.

For instance, Amazon believes putting people first, with a commitment to federal minimum wage at the top of their values, in addition to respecting LGBTQ rights. Apple upholds "accessibility" as the foremost value, creating products that are accessible to all, which in turn greatly promotes the development of functional applications for disabled and special groups population. Microsoft defines its mission as to empower every organization and individual to always achieve more with concrete actions in innovation, AI, trusted computing and other specific solutions.

As we can see, for corporations as well as individuals, it is imperative that before setting out a plan, to define what is your own *must do* mission.

Second. Inspiration.

It is hard to imagine a future out of nothing — this is where creative thinking tools comes in handy.

During thought experiments, we often brainstorm together and use special tools to stimulate imagination, help us project and express ideas. There are many ways to inspire, including visual, auditory, kinesthetic, verbal, scripted, spatial, tactile, olfactory. Depending on the context, a particular methodology will then be chosen.

At Maker Faire, solely through visual inspiration, we helped many participants to express their hopes and concerns on the future in a mere 10 to 20 minutes.

Here, I would like to share a few selected works:

From a 4-year-old: in the future, there will be robot companions to go Disneyland with, and kids don't have to worry about getting lost in the park anymore.

From a 5-year-old: I wish future hospital will be full of flowers, so kids won't get scared.

An 8-year-old's curiosity: What would sprout if humans take seeds from earth to plant on other planets?

A 10-year-old's hope: the future world should apologize to those who tried really hard but still suffered.

From an 18-year-old, who just step into adulthood: how do people hold on to their individual uniqueness in the future?

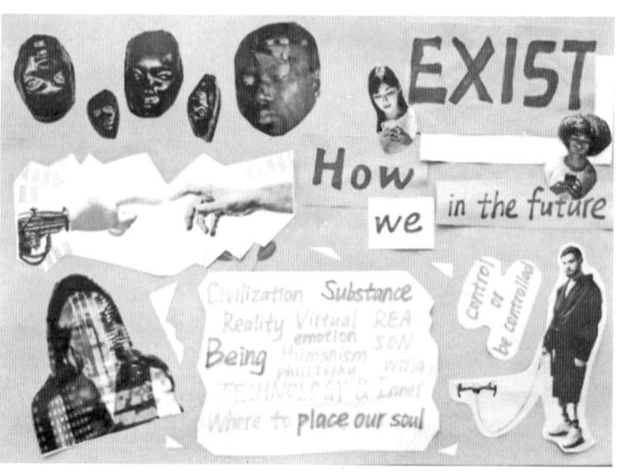

Inspiring people to discover their true thought with a clarified imagination, it turns out, is really not that difficult.

Needless to say that in addition to defining future values and inspiring creative thinking, the third most important thing is to be able to execute practical planning. That said, definition, inspiration, and execute will not be focused on in the book.

Instead, we will start from the very beginning — when the first questions are raised, and only then, step by step, will we look to inspire more thoughts and actions.

Before we set sail, let's wish that

In a forward march, nothing stops the brave.

Linna Zhao
22nd November, 2021

Preface

About the **Producer**

About the Producer: Wavemaker

Wavemaker is an innovative media agency that is affiliated with WPP — the world's largest advertising company, and media investment company GroupM. As a new communication agency, we inform to inspire, provoke to progress, and always relate ourselves to the future with both audacity and prudence. We analyze trends and predict the next hallmarks of commercial value for a diverse clientele. While constantly reinventing the industry by challenging conventionality and reimagining creativity, we never forget to heed the past to gain insights into the future and in so doing, bring our clients unique perspectives to achieve better tomorrows.

We believe that the paths to future is never singular. Working extensively with experts from a wide range of professions, from social scientists to tech entrepreneurs, we have come to believe that the most fundamental of all is the courage, curiosity, and commitment to raise a simple *what, why, how, what if ...* the list goes on. This otherwise inconspicuous act makes the world of

difference in enabling us to achieve wonders previously undreamed of, discover marvels hidden in plain sights, and most importantly, to indulge the first moment of curiosity and to ask more and more questions which eventually materializes the probable into the livable.

This book is such an attempt to combine practicality with imagination in molding into shape ten feature vignettes — each sketching a future in irreversible symbiosis with different transformative digital technologies that nonetheless are lived by ordinary people, to provoke you not only to calculate, to rationalize, but to relate to the future in ways that you might not do otherwise.

We hope that throughout the journey, you will join us in imagining, come to feel the human side of the ongoing technological overhaul of our social fabrics, and eventually, walk away with more questions than answers, curiosities than formulae about what will become of us.

About the Producer: Zhihu

Zhihu — with each question, there awaits answers.

Well known for its quality content and original users, Zhihu was officially launched in January 2011 with the brand mission to better knowledge and experience sharing, to help each one find their own answers.

In a letter to employees on 15 October 2010, Zhihu founder ZHOU Yuan expressed his intention in creating the platform:

We believe that on a litter-inundated Internet, information with real value is a true rarity. Knowledge — systematically organized high quality information — so far exists only in the minds of individuals in cyberspace, yet to be effectively mobilized en masse. What Zhihu offers, in this sense, is a tool to produce, share, and disseminate knowledge. We encourage everyone to share their knowledge, and by doing so, we are creating a meaningful collectivity for previously scattered bits and pieces of knowledge so they can be fully utilized for the public good.

Over the years, with its professional and friendly communities, unique structure, and easily accessible quality content, Zhihu has attracted highly dynamic groups of users, including those from the creative industries such as tech, business, film, fashion, culture, etc. As such, the site has witnessed all sorts of otherwise unimaginable curiosities that give unique insights into the contemporary Chinese psyche.

As of December 31, 2020, Zhihu accumulated 43.1 million content creators and has contributed 353 million pieces of content, including 315 million questions and answers. Every day, there are more than

20 million pieces of creation and interaction newly added on this platform. Zhihu's diversified content covers more than 1000 vertical fields and 571,000 different topics.

Currently, on top of the more traditional services and products such as question-and-answer communities, membership perks, search engines, topics board, etc., Zhihu also provides access to multimedia outlets including via image, video, and live stream to help people connect to the platform anywhere and anytime.

Since 13 January 2021, to better reflect Zhihu's belief in the future over a post-pandemic horizon, its slogan has been updated from "with each question, Zhihu awaits" to "with each question, there awaits answers".

Why We Wrote **this Book**

Live the moment!
Enjoy the wine today and leave the worries till tomorrow!
Carpe Diem!
Exclamation. Used to urge someone to make the most of the present time and give little thought to the future.

Since ancient times, we have attached great importance to the present, with striving hard and cherishing life seem to both exist in the present.

In the Western, tucked away in an obscure corner of history for nearly two millennia, *Carpe Diem* was catapulted overnight into the limelight by Robin Williams' electric performance in *Dead Poets Society*. The Latin phrase, which roughly translates into *seize* or *pluck the day*, was quickly pounced on by a ready public as *the* mantra of the day.

Live every day as your last, intoned enthusiasts, *let tomorrow's worry be tomorrow's.*

Indeed, why not? The approaching start of the third millennium will be, by many accounts, a fairly promising one. International commerce

was booming, unlocking ever more technological progress at a historically unmatched rate, to which much of our lives were rapidly outsourced, freeing up more spaces for personal pursuits.

When life is surely getting better, we also believe that rapid development of science and technology in the right direction will bring much more betterment to more people in the future. As such, the future started to lose its once tantalizing, often unsettling hold on our imagination, and instead became a thing of comfort because we knew that upon waking up the next morning, more machines would be manufactured, algorithms written, with the explicit purpose of taking care of more problems that we would have to otherwise address ourselves. Unknown but no longer uncertain, *future* was on its way to be written off as a thing to be solved sooner or later, so why would we be preoccupied by it anymore?

Admittedly, whether you like it or not, surprises often appear expectedly or unannouncedly in life, much to our chagrin, in the ensuing decades, time and again we were reminded of just what price we must pay for underestimating this temporal unknown while overindulging in the hopes that something will solve it all in our stead. Repetitive financial crises, disease outbreaks, armed conflicts, forced displacements — and as if not enough, the COVID-19 pandemic, through which we all experienced what impacts an uncertain future could bring.

Although future is not 100% predictable, it does not stop us to imagine and ensure that it is better in our hands.

That said, it would be imprudent to remain complacent and let technologies run their own courses. We need to start wonder more. We must ask ourselves not only *how did we get here,* but more importantly, *what must we do to remain true to our bold adventure*

onto a better path? In short, we need to start asking ourselves more questions.

Even though it is not difficult to come up with questions as human beings are born to be questioners, it is nonetheless not easy to continuously push ourselves to do so, as this too, ironically, has in the meantime become something of a luxury for many of us. There seem to be more things to worry and less to be curious about. Plus, the unprecedented breakthroughs in technological progress — especially for those living in cities, for whom life has become convenient and comfortable to such an extent that a considerable portion of everyday life is already tasked to a machine or an algorithm somewhere. As a result, we are falling into the trap of believing in progress for the sake of progress, all the while forgetting along the way how to be curious about our path to the future.

We have to wake up from the lulling comfort of taking things for granted and to provoke those who are still struggling to reimagine tomorrow as something radically different into questioning the nature of their realities. At the same time, we need to ensure that our own technological inventions remain the force by which we create a better tomorrow together. In other words, to live in a future that is more inclusive, efficient and sustainable, we need to challenge the ways in which we have been doing things until now, to relearn how to be curious, imaginative, bold, innovative, and most critical of all, to take that first step in raising questions — however simple — about both the known and unknown.

We believe that what brought us so far, what define *who* we are, is the very genuine curiosity and countless questions behind it. For it is these unfeigned utterances that inspire us to record histories, and in time, with tenacity, land us where we are going to be.

Few More Words
from the Editor

I'm not the writer of this book. Indeed, this book is a co-creation piece by many different people.

In writing this book, we selected widely different questions, talked to people from a diverse range of background, consulted experts from various industries — all to make our readers become more curious, to ask more questions.

This work would not have come into being without my colleagues and friends at Wavemaker, as well as the team behind Zhihu. From a wide range of professions, at different stages in life, they all contributed tremendously to the becoming of this project by having the passion as well as commitment to constantly look forward, to imagine, question, and seek for answers that are not easily within reach.

From the Wavemaker team, I am deeply indebted to Gordon Domlija, Jose Campon, Ann Lim, Henry Wang, Hadassah Chen, Roy Zhang, Lisa Dai, Lynn Lin, Bin Hu, Louis Zheng, Talise Zhou, Rio Liu, Katy Sun, Chloe Zhao, Yulie Zhu, Zaida Cai, Kelvin Lau, Patty Shao, Vikas Lin whose dedication to envisioning a better future over the years I've had the privilege of knowing them influenced me

greatly.

In particular, I'd like to express my gratitude to Charlotte Wright, for her frank feedback in pushing the limits of this narrative to its current parameters; and to Nic McCarthy for her support in setting a more poetic tonality for this book; I'd also like to send my special thanks to Jeffrey Wang, who helped us reimagine the English version of this story, in addition to introducing in general, a bit more flavor.

And my special thanks to Zhihu team, whose determined quest to perfect the art of questioning inspired me immensely.

And the Users on Zhihu, who generously shared their bold questions with us to the identified 10 scenarios.

With humility and once again, gratitude to all those who contributed to bringing this book to life, we share with you the questions that keep us awake at night and day alike — many of which inevitably lead to ponderings about what awaits us in those uncharted temporal frontiers. Needless to say, to answer all the questions that are raised in the following pages is simply beyond the scope of this book. What we look to achieve, instead, is to persuade and provoke you to join us in thinking and raising questions about a time in space yet to be mapped, a shared future towards which we trek together. We hope our questions are provoking enough for you to start questioning the conventional wisdom of *Carpe Diem*, and our imaginations sketched with sufficient clarity to draw your curiosity to the endless possibilities of the countless tomorrows.

Linna Zhao

Shanghai, 2021

Our Poem and Letters
to You

Zhihu's Poem about the future:

Time brings its own challenges,

in ways that few of us can foretell.

Cautious optimism, pressing challenges.

In an age when progress compressed, the once
time-honored wisdom

on truth, happiness, challenges

obsolete,

some of us lost, some confused,

yet for our generation, this is we have had,

and this will be our future.

Our optimism once innocent,

ourselves now trekking

through strange and uncharted terrains,

with no footprints to follow,

no road marks about whereto.

Where are we going? We ask.

But the echoes drift back to us,

unanswered.

It appears, we will have to chart this uncertain terrain

on our own.

44 million questions, 240 million answers.

From the cosmic to the microscopic,

this is our curiosity, guiding us

at this uncertain time.

Through words, pictures, videos,

in fear in anxiety, with pride with prejudice,

we marched on, undaunted,

into the heart of the unknown.

Between a question and an answer,

we,

only yesterday perfect strangers,

are lighting this undiscovered path

together

for the curious, for the desperate, for you and

me,

an arm’s length at a time,

hand in hand,

bringing illumination to all

who dare to follow.

At the beginning, they say,

there was no road.

And we,

in this adventure into the future,

are the authors

of our own tales.

We believe

there are never enough questions,

and we believe

every question, however asked,

will bring light,

solace,

curiosity to

someone who

is on the same journey as yourself.

The challenges of our time

will have to be answered,

and will be answered

by us.

With each question, there awaits answers.

A letter from **Wavemaker**

Gordon Domlija

CEO, Wavemaker APAC

A person who is passionately committed to my personal motto "Always towards better things".

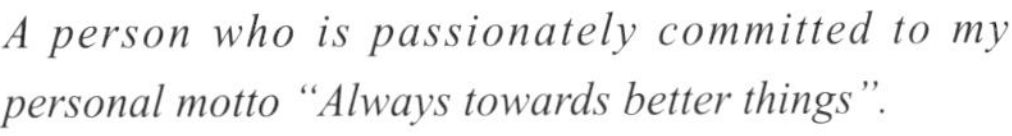

THE FUTURE HAD ARRIVED. THINKERS HAVE SET OUT.

The world changed forever in 2020. No matter who you are or where you are from, the pandemic has changed your future. No event in history has ever had its impact felt so broadly and so deeply. The only certainty we all now face is that nothing we know can be taken for granted, and nothing in the future can be certain.

As with any change in circumstances, at any scale, some are left feeling perplexed, some are

poised, some falter, some prosper. Each individual and enterprise need to rely on their own resilience and readiness to determine how successfully they are to navigate their own future.

The most prepared enterprises and individuals have accelerated their speed of transformation, re-examining the present and thinking about how to embrace and harness change.

While 2020 will be remembered for only one thing, we have also witnessed the first year of 5G, an expanding internet of everything, edge computing, financial technology, cashless economies, ban on plastics and decarbonization. This all point us with optimism to what the future could look like.

The world in science fiction stories seems surreal and improbable, yet in reality the "future" always arrives silently. Because of this, many individuals and enterprises miss the deep thinking and planning required for future growth. Our task is to ensure that you are prepared to succeed.

The future has arrived, thinkers have already set out.

Jose Campon
CEO, Wavemaker China

Passionate and driven by endless curiosity, in the believe that it will make our lives far more interesting.

WE CAN ONLY CHANGE FOR BETTER NO MATTER WHAT

Nobody has a crystal ball. There is always something that we just simply cannot even imagine, as much as we try.

In Spain, there is a saying that "the only thing we know about the future is that in 100 years it will be there".

Although there is always a difficult moment or moment of loss, and still many things to worry about, like divides, illness, social issues, etc., but this is what life is about, right? To experience the experiment waiting for us. Humans always have a set of feelings. Those feelings are not your identity. The feelings are just chemistry.

Particularly in China, there is nothing to lose, but everything to win. There is this very positive spirit and willingness to do things and not being afraid of the future. There is an embrace of technology that is not seen in the west. Look at Amazon. Amazon has built an advertising product which they did not have before. But they have a

marketplace now after learning from the Alibaba model. Another startup that I'm paying attention to recently is Shein, a Chinese company transforming the supply chain completely in fast fashion industry, with designing and producing on the spot.

I believe, the future is about Openness. It is about all the possibilities that tear down the constraints that you build around yourself from the past.

Even if everything can happen, there are emerging things that we can expect.

I've changed my life and who I am many times before. Even if sometimes I didn't think that I was going to be able to change. So, you think about yourself, have an image of yourself, then, gain a new identity of yourself.

Come and see, open your mind. You will always experience a journey of enriching yourself, opening your mind, seeing possibilities that are here for you.

We can only change for better.

Henry Wang

Chief Product Officer, Wavemaker

An enthusiast in finding the balance between foresight and action.

LET OUR CURIOSITY DRIVE PROGRESS

How many people 100 years ago imagined that the internet would change the world? Did any chess player 50 years ago believe that a machine could beat a Chess Master within 10 years? No one had imagined as recent as 4 years ago that a Chinese company developed social media app such as TikTok would win over young people around the world!

There is an unaccountable number of things that have happened in this world throughout history that have led us to where we are today. Especially right now because of the rapid acceleration in the information technology industry (and their salespeople!). It may seem as though the science fiction world is already upon us. But really, can we say that that is the case? Don't get me wrong, today the world is full of wonders, but can we still accurately predict something as "simple" as the weather two weeks out? Furthermore, very few had predicted the COVID-19 pandemic before it actually happened

last year.

The point is not to say that the science fiction world is unrealistic, but rather, the idea is to highlight that this is all but a part of a grand journey. If the science fiction utopia is to be conceived as the endgame of our journey, let's not assume we have successfully completed 90% of it and everything from now on will simply happen automatically as predicted. We are most likely still, at best, 50%, and the remaining voyage will rely very much on a combination of machines taking care of efficiencies while us humans continuing to take brave new steps to create and to innovate.

Thus, curiosity is as important as it had always been. There are so many predictions of the future, we can now test new ideas much more quickly as never before. It will all come down to imaginative minds that continue to push the boundaries of what is possible.

There are questions
from other Wavemaker
buddies raised to you

About life and work

Vikas : What will we waste on with time “saved” by technology?

Zaida : Will we need someone to do the household chores?

Patty : Where will we work in most of the time and how will the colleagues collaborate with each other?

Kelvin : Will the technology empower or replace us?

Tony : Will future technology squeeze the value of people?

Linna : Will everyone fight for their passion?

About peace, love, and relationship

Rose : Will there be better ways to resolve disputes in the future?

Linna : Will people in the future have greater goodwill toward the world and creatures?

Katy : Will the bond among friends and families become weaker?

Linna : How are we going to maintain our core relations and networks?

About population, the Earth and the universe

Chloe : Will the global population drop dramatically due to aging and low birth rate?

Arts : Will the average life expectancy be 100? What does the future old life look like?

Emily & Chloe : Will the globalization move forward or backward?

Kelvin : Will the world become borderless?

Yulie : Will technology widen the gaps between people and countries?

Zaida : Will technology cause gap of wealth? Will the age of cyberpunk arrive?

Arts : Will the pollution be solved in the future? Will there be less vegetation? Will the iceberg melt completely? Will rare species become extinct?

Emily : Will the Earth resources be exhausted ?

Chloe : Will we meet aliens in the future?

Rose : Will we find the second home in the universe?

About consumption & transportation

Zaida : Will offline stores still exist in the future? If they exist, how will their roles change?

Zaida : When the currency is fully digitized, how will it affect the existing online payment world?

Patty : Will the road transportation become more efficient with the popularization of automatic driving?

Tony : Will there be roads that can charge electric cars?

So, let's start with questions to imagine the future!

Contents

I Opening: Terraforming the Unknown

Progress does not always come without unintended consequences. The clock is ticking, stratosphere thinning, wildfires raging — the question that inspired and haunted Gauguin, in our time, has assumed an urgency unlike ever before. Where are we going?

Let's start with four questions and to think about the future!

1. What does it mean to be Human?
Human Augmentation ---------- *009*

2. Are we becoming more or less connected with each other?
Between and Betwixt: The Promises and Ambiguities of Hyperconnectivity ---------- *010*

3. Are we the sum total of our data?
Cybersecurity and Data Ownership ---------- *011*

4. Where is technology taking us? And who is directing technology?
Democratizing Technology ---------- *013*

Ⅱ 10 Future Life Scenarios

Based on concrete technological and humanistic trends, we outline what future life could look like with easily relatable scenarios. At the same time, we share our optimistic predictions and raise critical questions about the future, while keeping an eye on business inspirations and marketing opportunities.

1. Future Travel 017-025

Questions from Zhihu:

If space travel is to become available to the public, what issues remain to be solved, how can they be tackled?

With Doraemon's time machine, when period do you want to visit?

Our Questions:

What is the ultimate meaning of travel? And does its boundary only lie in time, space, and culture?

Keywords of future travel trend

Barrier-free Travel Overcoming language and cultural barrier, exploring the unknown without constraints

Virtual Wormhole Navigating between time and space

2. Future Growth (1) —Talents 026-035

Questions from Zhihu:

After further integration of the digital and the mechanical, how will human intelligence progress?

When everybody becomes omnipotent, what will we further pursue?

Our Questions:
Will we realize more life value in the future? And will we be happy then?

Keywords for Future Growth (1) — Talent Trend

Super π-Shaped Talents All-round talent + multi-field expert

2. Future Growth (2) —Learning *036-043*

Questions from Zhihu:
If you could learn a truly difficult thing in one day, what would you want to learn the most?
Will physical schools disappear in 20 years?

Our Questions:
How can future learning balance bottom-up self need with top-down "must learn" content? For instance, cultural inheritance, moral civilization, etc.

Keywords for Future Growth (2) — Learning Trend

Humanized experiential learning More customized learning for individuals

3. Future Work *044-052*

Questions from Zhihu:
What will be left to the humans after AIs replace most known work?
In the future where work-life boundary becomes unintelligibly blurred, how do we lead a good life?

Our Questions:

In the future, how will the form and mode of work be transformed? What kind of work form is the best form to reach work-life balance?

Keywords of future work trend

Integration of Work and Life

Work Imitates Life vis-à-vis Life Imitates Work

Digital Nomads: work across space and time

Free choice of workspace, circumvent conventional spatial limits

4. Future Entertainment *053-062*

Questions from Zhihu:

Will the Metrix become reality one day?

If two certified, highly competitive future-forecasters were to play rock paper scissors, who would win?

Our Questions:

In the future, will entertainment still be like "entertainment"? And will we still be participants or take the lead in our own entertainment experience?

Keywords for future entertainment trend

To Immerse or Not to Immerse — Connect anytime anywhere to immersive experiences

Emotional Immersion — Participate and lead, unfold your own story

5. Future Consumption *063-071*

Questions from Zhihu:

Is there a place in the future for physical stores?
How will sustainable products influence future consumerism?

Our Question:

In the future, how can we balance rationality and emotion to make consumption decision that generates the highest value?

Keywords of future consumption trend

A Thousand Hamlets in a Thousand People's Eyes	Personalized or customized shopping experience
Shoplaying	Experiential retail, diversifying choices

6. Future Home *072-081*

Questions from Zhihu:

How will future homes be designed and developed?
How will traditional Chinese family structure change in the coming decades?

Our Question:

What will home be defined as in the future?

Keywords of future home trend

Home+	A multipurpose home
Smart Family Members	Smart butler

7. Future Community 082-093

Questions from Zhihu:

In the next decade, what changes will technological advancement bring to our communal lives?
Will co-living become mainstream?

Our Question:

Will the future community help realize what life should be like?

Keywords of Future Community Trend

Ecologizing Community

More multifunctional and socio-ecologically sustainable community centers

8. Future Health 094-103

Questions from Zhihu:

Can future medicine completely eradicate myopia?
Has Forward Head Posture (FHP) already become a trademark of modern humans? In what ways can it be prevented?

Our Question:

In the future, can we more easily manage the health of ourselves and our families at different stages of life?

Keywords of future health trend

Smart Health Management

A comprehensively designed healthcare industry covering all life stages

9. Future Social Life 104-113

Questions from Zhihu:

Can social phobia, or social anxiety disorder, be alleviated in virtuality?

If you are given the choice to have virtual nationalities, what kind of virtual country do you dream of joining?

Our Question:

In the future, how will more complex social relationships and multiple identities broaden the width of our lives?

Keywords of future socid life trend

Multiple Selves in Parallel Worlds Different identities for different space

10. Future Data Asset 114-123

Questions from Zhihu:

How can data help us better review the past, or inspire the future?

Will immortality without corporeal appendage become reality if all information stored in the brain could be converted into uploadable data?

Our Question:

Will our data become an asset or a burden of redundancy?

Keywords of future data trend

Data Becoming Asset Personal data become asset with legally protected ownership

Epilogue *125*

I

Opening: Terraforming the Unknown

Where do we come from?
What are we?
Where are we going?

Not long after Charles Darwin published his theories on evolution, French painter Paul Gauguin, in a Tahiti still pristine from overtourism, set down his canvas and painted the famous work titled with the thrice searing questions. At a time when the theory of natural selection was still viewed with outright hostility on one end to flippant disbelief on the other, Gauguin's painting posed an existential interrogation to a post-Enlightenment public, still lost in the wonders they had achieved since the industrial revolution and looked at the world with insouciance, ready to do what they pleased with it.

In China, our culture attaches great importance to "roots", and has been very accustomed to and naturally concerned about the question of "where we came from". We emphasize inheritance and worship our ancestors. We recite 5000 years' long history with great honor. This is indeed the very important fact that makes me so proud of our country.

However, when it comes to the question of "where are we going", it seems to have entered a slightly blurry area. Our culture appreciates the "golden mean" and the spirit of broad love, as well as the spirit of diligence, unity and hard work. The future seems more like an attitude towards life.

By the sunken barge a thousand sails go past. Before the withered tree all trees go green in spring.

When you hoist the sails to cross the sea,you'll ride the wind and cleave the waves.

No fear of destiny.

The eagle strikes the sky, the fish shuttles the river, and everything competes for freedom

The past and present seem to have always received relatively more attention than the future.

In the Western world, more than a hundred years later, after two catastrophic world wars, countless smaller scale conflicts, droughts, famines, disease outbreaks, we the *Homo Sapiens* of the 21st century have a rather good idea of where do we come from and what are we. But one question remains, *where are we going*? In other words, what future awaits us?

From the boundless post-war optimism of *Star Trek* to the stereotypical technoir dystopia of *Blade Runner*, the future has always meant different things at different times — more or less oscillating between hope and hopelessness. More recently, however, it appears that the pendulum has become rather stuck. The unprecedented speed of progress brought by digital technologies

seemed to have lulled many of us into a complacent stupor to probe beyond the next iPhone release or Netflix hit — attention span cut ever shorter by social media, eyes glued to a screen that always has the next swipe waiting, our faith in a positively better future by the inherent merit of technology has become akin to a kind of religious faith, almost a fundamentalism.

Alarmingly, just like the market fundamentalism that spawned crushing crises and wrecked livelihoods without warning, this widespread belief that technology will solve all the problems itself created, as remarks from historian and writer Ronald Wright, *has become very similar to the religious belief that caused some societies to crash and burn in the past.* The future, warns Wright, is not always better. And progress not always without unintended consequences.

The clock is ticking, stratosphere thinning, wildfires raging — the question that inspired and haunted Gauguin, in our time, has assumed an urgency unlike ever before.

Where are we going?
What is future?

From the plains of precolonial America to classical Athens, vastly different versions of the future are induced, imagined, invoked, and finally, immortalized. Be it via peyote vision or dionysiac stupor, in the form of cave painting or staged tragedy, humans have always co-existed with time — past or ahead, in a singularly nonlinear fashion.

The English word for future comes from the Latin *futurus*, future participle of *esse*, which in a literal sense means *to be*, or *going to be*. Half a world away, the Chinese civilization had a rather different, perhaps less certain attitude when looking at things, present or

otherwise.

The modern Chinese word for the present in the future — (wèi lái) — literally means something that has not yet come, which is more consistent with the West. But in our bones, we are much more practical. The expressions of the future in ancient China are mostly relatively recent dates, such as the coming future (after now), tomorrow morning, tomorrow, the coming day, etc. This is a very practical and interesting cultural consensus and mentality. We seem to care more about the closer date that can be promised or planned. The slightly distant "future" which is full of changes seems to be absent in our consciousness. "What we can catch now" will always get more attention than "what the future will need".

For what it's worth, the future, notwithstanding linguistic and other disagreements between civilizations on what it actually is, is at the end of the day, not a *to be or not to be* conundrum for human beings on planet Earth. With each planetary rotation we inch forward in time, elapsing moments of countless yesterdays transcribed into memory, or discarded along the way, all the while leaving our increasingly indelible marks in time and space. It seems that we are rather caught up in a vortex and into the future — with certainty or trepidation — is the only way to go.

Yuval Harari writes in *Homo Deus: A Brief History of Tomorrow* that as the three main issues that confronted humanity throughout much of recorded history — war, hunger, disease — seem to have all but disappeared in certain parts of the world and on track of disappearing in others, we are potentially facing another *the-end-of-history* moment, namely, what will our new preoccupation be in a century that is, by and large, the most prosperous ever throughout

human existence?

Then, do you still wish to know about the future?

To be or not to be, that is the question. But to ask or not to ask is, at least to children, not much of a choice after all.

Before reaching their fifth year on this strange planet, children, observes Warren Berger in *A More Beautiful Question*, ask an average of 40,000 questions. It is through formulating burning curiosity into tangible questions that we, in our apprenticeship of becoming human, attach meaning to people and objects, discover ourselves in the mirror for the first time, make sense of countless yesterdays, todays and tomorrows in this then alien world. But with each setting of the sun, routines settle in, occupying the moments that were used to be reserved for questioning and imagining, creating and recreating. The child becomes the adult, questions turn into answers.

Luckily, not all.

Throughout history, it is precisely this ability to ask trivial or daunting questions — with or without strict necessities — that brought us scientific breakthroughs and philosophical insights, it is this relentless curiosity in each of us that gave us hope and direction in moments of insurmountable hardship. Familiar or strange, packed with answers or blank as sheet, to wake up into an uncharted tomorrow, all we can be sure is that we will still ask on, unapologetically, as if it were the first time.

Since its launch ten years ago, more than 44 million questions have

circulated on Zhihu, asked by Chinese citizens from all walks of life, on topics from the microscopic to the cosmic. Each of them beckoned an answer, inviting, intriguing, insisting us to take one more step in thought, to join whoever raised it to think, to answer, and to ask. Like its millions of users, Zhihu believes that to step into the future, there is no better way than to be brave and ask questions with or yet without answers.

At Wavemaker, we have always asked tough questions about the future to our people, to our clients, and to our partners, to not only live it tomorrow, but to foresee and understand it today. We are firm believers and practitioners that the future, as uncertain as it is, without exception originates in our past deeds, and at the end of the day, it is our insatiable curiosity that has directed and decided countless tomorrows in the vast expanse of history.

Together, we explore a future in which human and technology have become unprecedentedly interconnected, at a time when we are witnessing irreversible, albeit deeply paradoxical decoupling with each other.

Will the utopian dreams since Thomas More's time be realized one day? Or will the Matrix become fact instead of fiction?

Not all the questions lead to clear answers. But with each answer, there certainly be questions driven by curiosity.

For now, we will explore the future by asking questions that are fundamental to our being in this present century and to explore, to envision how by the simple act of asking, we could come to see, to understand, to feel the future, and perhaps with luck, even to live it in our imagination, one step ahead of time.

1. What does it mean to be Human?

Human Augmentation

What defines our limitations? Nature or nurture?

In different cultures, there are fantasies about the limits and super abilities of human body.

Will future humans have access to the physical strength of Sun Wukong or Thor and the mental fortitude of Vulcans? Will linguistic barrier between peoples be dissolved by the click of a button? Will our progeny be endowed with wings, night visions, gills, as Epimetheus — the Greek god who was tasked with creating beasts from the same clay that humans were molded into being — forgot to give us?

In the tittering amphitheaters of the ancient Greeks, to be human is to be the mortal plaything of capricious gods and goddesses, visited upon by cruel fate even after the most glorious victories over one's nemesis. Under the sunless future Californian sky of Philip K. Dick's *Do Androids Dream of Electric Sheep*? popularly known by its film adaption, Ridley Scott's *Blade Runner*, to be human is to exist in frictionless synthesis with invasive, mechanical implants, and to live side by side with impeccable androids that could hardly be told from actual humans.

In the 20 years of entering the 21st century, although there has been no significant progress. However, Human augmentation, or the utilization of technologies that enhance existing human bodily (physical and mental) capabilities, once more pushes those

questions to the forefront. Be it the chemical stimulants that increase attention control, the exoskeleton suits that help those with walking disabilities to walk again, or the VR goggles that relocate us into whole new holographic worlds, human augmentation will, and in many ways is already in the progress of, redefine yet again what it means to be human in the current century.

But mechanical symbiosis aside, how does pervasive technologies change the social aspect of being human in the Internet Age?

2. Are we becoming more or less connected with each other?

Between and Betwixt: The Promises and Ambiguities of Hyperconnectivity

As described by sociologist FeiXiaotong and Professor Ming-JerChen, guanxi can be visualised like the concentric ripples from a pebble hitting water, from the center(self) to those falling further to the center. The closer the circle is to the center, the closer their guanxi is. The most important relationship to us is still what's in the closer circle.

Today, surrounded by smart devices — some already are, in many ways, smarter than us — with their myriad of daily advice on virtually everything, we seem to be equally confused on what it means to genuinely connect with one another as our scientifically much less sophisticated ancestors were, if not more. The fact that to meet a stranger now for those who have internet access is but a

few clicks away does not tell us, unfortunately, how can we relate to, understand, feel and connect with those whom we pile onto our social media friend list.

Is falling hopelessly in love with a smart Operating System (OS), as Joaquin Phoenix's character did in Spike Jonze's 2013 film *Her*, a genuine connection? Or does it merely reflect the increasing inability of our over-customized generation to deal with fundamentally different others?

Today, a newborn child is more likely than ever to grow up into ways of sociality that are utterly unimaginable, if not outright nonsensical to their parents. The wisdom of the past is evidently falling behind in catching up with the present, let alone the future. Magic or not, we will have to navigate many tomorrows in which perhaps, the profile photos we see of each other on screens evoke more genuine feelings than the physical presence of their offline proprietors.

Will the real feeling under the hyperconnectivity and the alienation from reality make people fall into this fuzzy trap?

3. Are we the sum total of our data?

Cybersecurity and Data Ownership

Governments of the Industrial World, you weary giants of flesh and steel, I come from Cyberspace, the new home of Mind. On behalf of the future, I ask you of the past to leave us alone ... We will create a civilization of the Mind in Cyberspace. May it be

more humane and fair than the world your governments have made before.[1] From Davos, Switzerland, 1996, John Barlow and fellow internet enthusiasts proclaimed the independence of the newly commercialized Net with undaunted zeal and optimism. Little did they — or many of us at the time — know what was in store.

Successive scandals, leaks, and hacks in the 2010s vaporized any illusion that the Internet was a pristine frontier where we could start all over. Instead, public attention was galvanized on what had till then, largely been taken for granted by most, i.e., who have access to the data we generate, and how are they using it. With tech giants busy exploiting the ambiguity of data ownership and academics preoccupied debating over what does it mean to institute legal data rights, belatedly, more people have at last awoken to the dangers of lacking basic digital privacy or property infrastructure.

For better or for worse, an increasingly connected world in which our digital personae — and their footprints — play a more vital role than our physical presence in both work and leisure appears rather inevitable at this point, and we will have to accept the fact that however much we wish, cyberspace is decidedly not going to become a pure place of the mind any time soon. Quite on the contrary, the online will be, as it always has been, a highly dynamic, inclusive, often messy place, just like any place on this side of the screen. As such, are we willing to do what it takes to make it somewhere that is fairer, saner, and more humane?

---

1 A Declaration of the Independence of Cyberspace. The full document can be found at https://www.eff.org/cyberspace-independence.

4. Where is technology taking us? And who is directing technology?

Democratizing Technology

In his acclaimed 2002 book *Transforming Technology,* American philosopher Andrew Feenberg reminds us of the dangers of an advent modern priest class — the technology elites — who are bent on establishing a monopolistic order over new technologies and the dire consequences this would have on the rest of the world. Instead, he argues, the direction of future technologies should be open for all to participate and access, thus achieving real progress in the sense that technologies can become fully synergetic vis-à-vis their environment.

In many ways, this foretold the stories of the open source, open access, and many similar movements that had since become mainstream. With policy makers waking up to calls to place more emphasis on stakeholders instead of just shareholders, the trend to democratizing technology is rapidly transforming our societies in everyday life, from finance (cryptocurrency) to education (remote learning) to healthcare (Wuhan Pandemic Control in 2020), in ways that many of us still find pleasantly surprising.

What remains to be seen is, how are we directing this trend to build a better and more sustainable world?

Utopia or oblivion, progress or more of the same, the future is, after all, just another day that each one of us invariably wakes up to, with confidence or confusion, a smile or a frown. Like countless yesterdays we would walk under the same sky, traverse the same

stream of time in awe, in flippancy, try however we may to make sense and meaning out of the minutes and hours that imperceptibly slip past us.

The future, in other words, is us. And we are what we choose to or not to be. Today, with the ubiquity of digital technology, it is nearly impossible to live without some kind of cyborgish symbiosis, willingly or otherwise. What we choose to do with those technologies, on the other hand, is up to us.

Like you, we at Wavemaker and Zhihu are deeply concerned, hopelessly curious, and cautiously confident about what is yet to come. We believe that with foresight and diligence, boldness and responsibility, the future could be, on a fundamental level, more sustainable, efficient, convenient, and inclusive for all of us.

From the foot of the Colosseum to Beijing old Lanes, from a buoyant digital nomad to a septuagenarian old schooler, we invite you to join us in a journey into time, to imagine together what tomorrow means for the daily lives of you and me, how we might interact with the benefits brought by scientific progress and why not to, in the meantime, forget to look backwards and raise critical questions about the darker side of technology.

Without further ado, the future awaits. Are you ready to unfold the 10 future life scenarios on the next page?

II

10 Future Life Scenarios

1. Future Travel

Despite the fact that to a growing number of people, traveling has become an integral part of their lives, the plethora of technological enablers that emerged over recent years — from online travel agents (OTA) to simultaneous translation apps — do not seem to have improved their experiences much, largely due to language and/or cultural barriers, time constraints, and other difficulties. As a result, opportunities to delve deeper into authentic local history and community frequently leave them unfulfilled.

Our questions: **What is the ultimate meaning of travel? And does its boundary only lie in time, space, and culture?**

Prospect of Future Travel

The world is my oyster. Rome, here I come.

Rome, Italy

A friend once told me that the beauty of traveling by oneself is to be free to choose among the unknown, and to feel the spontaneity that is the essence of those unchartered moments.

As the plane descended over this ancient city, my smart glasses started zooming in on the neatly compartmentalized countryside, showing me grape varieties of different vineyards, knowing my enthusiasm for wine. In lieu of the slight panic that I thought I would be experiencing, I felt instead tinges of irrepressible excitement, if not impatience to start exploring already.

For someone who spoke no Italian, my travel kit was my personalized guide — the EarPods narrated fascinating drama behind every magnificent church or humble store I walked past, which was simultaneously captured and road marked by my glasses. Even for street musicians, it could tell me the exact songs they played, not forgetting

to remind me to leave a tip.

After walking around the Colosseum, I decided that the actual edifice — magnificent as it was — could satisfy my curiosity no longer. Sitting down on a quiet spot on the top rows, I selected several historical files from the cloud via my glasses, tapped download, and voilà! In the blink of an eye, right there under the same capricious sky, in front of my unquenchable excitement, the spectacular life-and-death struggles of the unfortunate, the breath-taking duels of celebrity gladiators were recreated to the last minute detail by the built-in AR features of the glasses. Having already seen this countless times on screen, I was still shocked to the core when I looked around and, amidst incomprehensible shouting from a virtual crowd, saw the raw barbarity of ancient Romans, the mirthless death orders their nobles tossed out by a simple gesture, and all of a sudden appreciated my luck to be born into a civil, peaceful time all the more.

Having had a taste of that ancient excitement, I decided it was time to find a cosy, anonymous bistro for lunch. After half an hour of indecision (they all looked wonderful!), I finally decided to walk into one that seemed to be carefully tucked into the heart of a labyrinthian district. Thanks to my glasses, the Italian menu was instantly translated, while the waiter's friendly greetings were dubbed into Chinese by the EarPods simultaneously as he spoke — albeit his Italian sounded much more charming than the AI generated Chinese translation!

Looking back on the trip, quite as I expected, the solitary journey did not feel lonely at any turn. In addition to the spontaneous joys from exploring the unknown, my high-tech travel kit felt as though a sentient guide — or a companion even — throughout the days. With it, the world is my oyster, and who knows where to next?

Keywords of future travel trend

What we believe the future travel will look like:

Barrier-free Travel

Overcoming language and cultural barrier, exploring the unknown without constraints

With real-time translation and cultural hints provided by AI, travelers could communicate with locals without previous hindrances, further enabling them to delve deeper into the layers of local culture that otherwise might remain inaccessible to conventional tourists. At the same time, Location-based Service (LBS) trackers record the journey down to the last detail, providing comprehensive safety guarantees.

Virtual Wormhole

Navigating between time and space

Immersive Virtual Reality (VR) and Augmented Reality (AR) technologies enable us to *be* anywhere, *feel* anything, free from spatial and temporal constraints. Via highly detailed interactive features, AR and VR users could, on top of merely spectating historical or future events, become active

participants and impact the trajectories of fictional timelines that *feel* no less real than reality.

How does technology unlock this future?

5G and cloud enabled AI combined with LBS, smart recognition, AR/VR, and real-time translation technologies will be able to provide solutions to many challenges that are most common during traveling, such as communication issues, cultural barriers, etc., thus substantially improving travel experience.

Viewed in this light, apps that gained rapid popularity in recent times, such as mobile AR Emoji, real-time satellite navigation and Pokemon Go, offer but a glimpse to a more interactive future in which, supported by a mature 5G network, as well as currently nascent technologies such as immersive VR, will usher us into worlds beyond 2-dimensional screens and linear timelines with truly inexhaustible endings.

What are the places you want to travel but haven't summoned up the courage to go?

Optimistic anticipation and provocative critique about future travel

Potential Benefits:

Easier to materialize

Travel anytime and anyplace, circumventing material constraints such as illness and time shortage

More Rewarding Experience

Travel through time, visit different timelines and places with more interactive and immersive designs

---

More Local

Easier to delve deeper into local culture

Safer

Full digital record and tracking, safeguarding against unexpected accident

---

More Convenient

Barrier-free communication and comprehension

Easier to Relive

Permanently digitalized travel experience down to the last detail, easier to relive precious moments

Meanwhile ...

While technology makes travel more convenient, will the sense of mystery, the unannounced surprise and joy that we experience when visiting an unknown place be diminished, or even lost? Will "knowing too much" create another kind of assembly line travel mentality?

Will anyplace, anytime immersive technology render traditional destination-oriented traveling obsolete?

Questions from Zhihu:

If space travel is to become available to the public, what issues remain to be solved, how can they be tackled?

If time travel really exists, why haven't we been visited by anyone from the future?

Will space become a popular travel destination in the next two decades?

With Doraemon's time machine, which period do you want to visit?

What unknowns on Earth are still waiting to be explored?

Questions from Zhihu Expert:

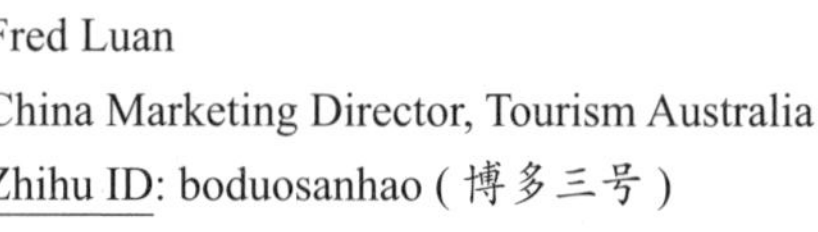

Fred Luan
China Marketing Director, Tourism Australia
Zhihu ID: boduosanhao (博多三号)

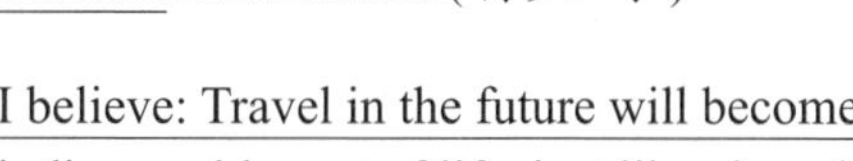

I believe: Travel in the future will become an indispensable part of life, just like air and water.

- Will there be an "anywhere door" in the future that you just need to get up and cross from home to wherever you want to go?
- Will the barriers of language, culture and nation be eliminated in the future so that people can walk around, get to know the residents, and immerse into local culture?
- Will future travelers pay more attention to differentiated experience than just to tick the to-go list with a fairly brief glance?

Mona Liu
Sales Director, Travel Agency mafengwo.com
Zhihu ID: Liu Naonao (刘闹闹)

I believe: Courage > Wisdom.

- Can space travel be fully commercialized?
- How will fundamental changes take place in future Online Travel Agency (OTA)?
- What new types of home stay will appear in the future?
- What sort of tourist destinations will become new popular in 20 years?

Provoking Future Opportunities:

Business Insights

- Develop tools that would bring travellers more convenient and smoother experiences, such as real-time translator, cross-culture travel guide (such as greetings, tipping practices, etc.);
- With the help of AR/VR, develop destination-related content and experiential scenarios to bring consumers more memorable travel experiences;
- Develop more virtual travel options and contents to inspire and help people explore online traveling;
- Provide non-intrusive tracking services to safeguard travel safety.

Marketing Insights

- Identify travel needs of different consumers across different contexts, and accurately build holistic communication methods. For instance, inspiring actual visit for destinations via virtual experiences, providing relevant products at critical junctures based on travel plans, and inspiring richer experiences at the actual destination;
- It will be necessary for multiple parties to jointly develop technologies and contents to improve travel experience, such as thematic and story-based plots;
- More types of theme tours and experiential tours will be created, with brands across different industries as vital promoters, helping consumers understanding brand cultures and values by experiential contents.

2. Future Growth(1) —Talents

Current changes in industrial structures and the emergence of new professions call for further diversification of human resources. A direct consequence of which is the rise of the T-shaped talents. In the meantime, the slash generation and freelancers are pushing a multi-expertise, multi-hobby trend into the mainstream, encouraging people to integrate personal choices into career planning, or even creating brand new work that are uniquely theirs.

With work from home becoming unprecedently prominent as a result of the ongoing pandemic, faster-paced work and life require considerably more efficiency to maintain. At the moment, countless efficiency tools are already beginning to be accepted by the public.

On the other hand, currently available high-techs have also begun to unleash our potentialities in terms of efficiency and creativity, making individuals more multifaceted. For instance, AI filters theoretically enables everyone to become photography pros, while the likes of AI writing and video editing offer more chances to those who wish to become folk artists.

Our questions: **Will we realize more life value in the future? And will we be happy then?**

Prospect of Future Growth (1) — Talent

Multi-job Life: My Career, My Choice

Letter from a finance news editor/vlogger.

As a finance news website editor/vlogger, I like to share financial knowledge and the lurid or tepid stories about money behind closed doors with my followers.

At first, I thought it was fairly easy to be a vlogger — after all, they all made it look all seem so effortless. But the moment I started recording and editing my first video, it dawned on me that this was a highly developed, ruthlessly demanding business. Not only were professional knowledge and constant research indispensable, one had to know how to fluently use an array of video editing softwares, plus necessary creative writing skills to convert dreary, unexcitable facts into contents that are interesting and relatable to different audiences — even if it included daily meme lessons — well, you get the picture.

Lucky for me, a friend recommended an AI assistance app, which boosted my creative efficiency in ways that I didn't expect at first. The app is fairly straightforward

to use: all I needed to do was to come up with a theme and a few keywords, hit the red button, and send it on its merry way, so to speak. The app filtered a humanly impossible amount of data from the cloud according to my query, and after finalizing on candidate materials, wrote first drafts that I could expand upon later. On the video front, it selected from the same cloud sources suitable pictures, while simultaneously picking appropriate background music, cut excerpts from all kinds of finance shows around the world and at last, composed a number of final candidates for me to choose from.

At this point, I have to admit that this AI assistance — which has saved me so much time and energy — is way better than a good number of professional teams. And this is my story on how I learned to stop worrying about limited resources and love technology!

Keywords for Future Growth (1) — Talent Trend

What we believe the future Travel will look like:

Super π-Shaped Talents

All-round talent + multi-field expert

Among existing professions, around half are either facing the prospect of being replaced by AI, or are already undergoing irreversible automation. With traditional work becoming increasingly scarce, new ones will be created in their place.

We need to be able to adapt to the different demands of future work.

Adaptability as such can come from transitioning to a π-shaped talent, which requires both breadth (a wide range of basic knowledge, multiple expertise and different capabilities) and depth (highly specific skills, commitment to a particular field, etc.).

A future like this requires much higher work efficiency along with different types of talents, and together, under technological progress, more time and energy can be freed up to do more meaningful things.

How does technology unlock this future?

Jobs that require highly specific professional skills, along with those that rely on precise communication, creativity, and decision-making will become mainstream work from which humans cannot be dismissed, whereas repetitive, labor-intensive work such as data collecting and processing will be compressed or completely automated. With the aid of efficiency tools and AI, people will be able to allocate more time to recreational activities which nonetheless can create social value that they are passionate about in the future, not to mention that AIs can also help us become better in our hobbies, so much so that we could become "professionals" in those fields.

On the creative front, the potentialities of AI could already be glimpsed: Microsoft Xiaoice, an AI system based on emotional computing framework, can compose poems and paint; the first portrait created by an AI was sold at Christie's for $432,500;

sci-fi writer CHEN Qiufan's AI software assisted novel won first place on the AI literary competition ... the list goes on. With the imminence of 5G network, AI artisticity will continue to extend to more creative venues that require faster internet and computing power, such as video streaming. Predictably, in the next 3 to 5 years, videos co-created by humans and AIs will become more popular.

At the same time, digitization is accelerating the integration of content industries, whereas future cloud storage will greatly enhance the capacity of data communication. Furthermore, the explosion of the sheer quantity of data will lead to continued upgrades in existing server capacity, while AI search functions based on 5G network will keep on improving the accuracy of search engines.

Sci-fi writer/Chen Qiufan

I used AI assistance with writing *The Algorithm of Life* in 2017.The interesting thing is, despite the apparent lack of logic among AI created sentences, they do have certain unique, inexplicable beauties. Those randomly generated materials brought me a good deal of inspiration.

More capabilities mean more possibilities. If realizable, what "superpower" do you want to have in the future?

Optimistic anticipation and provocative critique about Future Growth (1) — Talent

Potential Benefits:

More Efficient

Popularization of AI powered efficiency tools

Broader Horizon, Richer Experience

Cooperation with experts from different fields

More Professional

Continual accumulation of expertise and experience

More Career Choices

Presented with more opportunities across industries

More Purposeful in Life

Better career goals and plans

More Inclusive

Expertised in multiple professions

Easier to Succeed

Passionate about work choices

Meanwhile ...

Will the knowledge to fluently interact with and utilize AI technologies become basic skills for future populations? While such a professional lingua franca predictably brings increased efficiency and creativity, will reliance on it stifle human imagination?

With personal preference exerting an increasingly decisive impact on career choices, will it lead to the inundation of certain professions with an overabundance in human resources while critically depriving others?

Questions from Zhihu:

What are the limits of future psychological and physical development?

When everybody becomes omnipotent, what will we further pursue?

If you can have three superpowers, what will you choose?

After further integration of the digital and the mechanical, how will human intelligence progress?

Questions from Zhihu Expert:

Imin Pao
Founding Editorial Director of Vogue Business in China, President of PPGROUP & The Brand Partner
Zhihu ID: IminPao 包益民

I believe: Too busy planning for the future makes one forget living today.

- If you can travel back to 20 years ago and give yourself an advice, what would you say?
- How would you like to be remembered when you leave this world?
- What profession do you see yourself in if you no longer have to work for a living in the future?
- Quick, first reaction: your plane is going to crash, what is the first thing that comes to your mind?
- When you are passionate about something, you need to think what is the difference between love and herpes?

Michelle Jiang
Chief Talent Officer, GroupM
ZhihuID: MIMIMI (米米米)

I believe: Don’t hesitate, the future has come.

- What kind of talents does our society need in the future?
- In the future, will the talent differentiation in an organization become bigger or smaller?

- Will the future young generation still work and fight hard for what they will aim for?

Provoking Future Opportunities:

Business Insights

- Develop better smart devices, such as AI photography, editing or writing software, to further optimize work and help people become more professionally versatile;
- Develop vertical- or cross-field talent cooperation and exchange platforms to create more opportunities for collaboration and exchange between experts from different fields which increases professionalism in general, and brings more inspiration and creativity;
- Encourage balanced development, invest more strategically in industries that lack talent supplies.

Marketing Insights

- Basic market education and communication should be conducted for slash-enabling brands and products, with the aim of helping consumers to acquire more skills, such as tutorials for aerial photography amateurs;
- More precise matching between different talents the information they need, such as accurately providing more specialized learning content and communication opportunities for professionals in vertical fields;
- Forecast talent development through data and algorithm to

inspire future growth toward areas of interest;

- Transition brands into π-shaped ones as well to communicate with corresponding talents, who, on top of possessing professional expertise in the concerned industry, also have considerable knowledge in other related fields.

2. Future Growth(2) — Learning

At the moment, many public as well as private schools still rely on traditional spoon-feeding and standardized test-oriented educational models. However, pre-school educational institutes, including kindergartens, have started to experiment with alternative options that, with the help of AI technologies, make learning more customized, interactive, and fun. Meanwhile, teachers are exploring new ways of making courses more interesting, inspiring, and impactful.

On the other hand, with mandatory lockdowns, the current pandemic has pushed remote learning models — e.g., online classes (real-time or cloud based), "dual-tutor" (online+offline teachers), etc. — to the forefront of public discourse, which are quite likely to become mainstream in the near future.

Our questions: **How can future learning balance bottom-up self need with top-down "must learn" content? For instance, cultural inheritance, moral civilization, etc.**

Prospect of Future Growth (2) — Learning

Virtual Cast and Celebrity Director: A Scene across Two Dimensions

"More emotion in the eyes here."

"We need to shoot this closer."

"There needs to be more contrast between actors and the background."

At the flick of a switch, the dim room was suddenly flooded with light. In it, a few sophomores from the film department had been shuffling to and fro all day, learning and practicing virtual directing.

As they were preoccupied by the shooting, the AI tutor had already made extensive comments on each scene, from camera angle and lighting, to the actual acting. For now, the human professor was elaborating on this. In a typical filming class like this, every student could count on receiving constructive feedback on their works.

Today, the project was reshooting the ending for *In the Mood for Love*. State of the art AI and VR holographic technologies were used in the course, which accurately simulated professional actors that were in the movie by tapping into an acting data base that had complete records for past films. With this, students could handpick their ideal "virtual stars" and never worry about not being able to find proper actors when shooting individual projects.

This time, when Chow Mo-wan (virtual Tony Chui-Wai Leung) asked Su Li-zhen (virtual Maggie Cheung), "*If there's an extra ticket, would you go with me?*" Su *would say, "I will.*"

Keywords for Future Growth (2) — Learning Trend

What we believe the future travel will look like:

Humanized Experiential Learning

More customized learning for individuals

- Tailor-made education models that are based on student abilities and interests;
- Transforming education model: from spoon-feeding to immersive. Experiential learning to stimulate thinking and inspire learning.

How does technology unlock this future?

Aided by Artificial Intelligence, both formal education and home tutoring will become more efficient and personalized.

In schools, AI will become teaching assistants that customize learning plans for each student, develop corresponding curriculums, and allocate educational resources based on individual backgrounds, interests and aptitudes. At home, AI will be virtual tutors that can provide specifically designed lessons by acquiring suitable teaching materials from the cloud to best match each student's current capacities.

In the near future, with high-speed internet and latency-free computing brought by 5G, VR interactive experiences will become incrementally more natural, the advantage of which — including sandbox capabilities and simulation — aside from obvious commercial benefits for more entertainment oriented contexts, can be invaluable for educational purposes as well, especially when it comes to emergency drillings and universal basic education. Perhaps VR classes would emerge after current cloud classes, bringing more immersive and personalized learning experiences.

Virtual Technology Expert/Mr. L

The advantage of VR technology is that it is not confined by conventional physical limitation and can be carried as far as imagination can go. For educational purposes, it can be used for firefighting, military and other potentially dangerous training programs, while on the other hand, it can also relocate us into the heart of extremely macroscopic or microscopic worlds, such as out in space or inside individual cells.

Education Innovation Consultant/Candy

Project-based Learning (PBL) which is highly experiential-learning oriented, is in fact very costly and is not feasible to

be implemented on a large scale. If immersive learning can be realized by VR technologies, it could provide a direction for personalized education.

If customized courses and immersive learning are available, will you still see learning as a burden?

Optimistic anticipation and provocative critique about future Growth (2) — Learning

Potential Benefits:

More Fun

More interesting content, richer experience

Easier

Easier learning with AI assistance

More Customized

Big-data makes courses more tailor-fit to individual aptitudes

---

More Capable

Scientific and diverse learning methods cultivate student's critical thinking

---

Easier to inspire and motivate

Inspire and motivate students through optimized learning and teaching methods

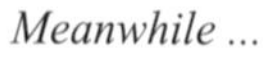

Meanwhile ...

Will over-customization make us too independent from each other, and lose necessary exchanges that are critical to healthy learning?

Will overreliance on algorithm induced stimulation dull individual initiativeness, reduce student curiosity and creativity?

Questions from Zhihu:

If you could learn a truly difficult thing in one day, what would you want to learn the most?

Will physical schools disappear in 20 years?

Questions from Zhihu Expert:

Qiwen Cui
Zhihu Social Innovation Lab/Bottle Dream
ZhihuID: CuiQiwen (崔绮雯)

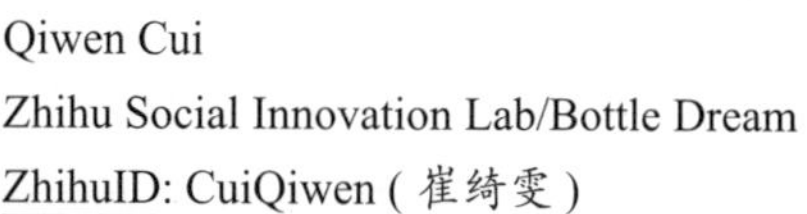

I believe: The future is based on our imagination.

- With the development of brain-computer interface and other related technologies, is it possible to “transfer” knowledge directly without “learning” in the future?
- Will artificial intelligence be our teacher in the future?

Cui Cui
Youshi University
ZhihuID: Youshi University（优势大学）

I believe: Future is inherently unpredictable. The only thing that one can rely on in a time like this is one's own advantages.

- Will future children know by heart their advantages from an early age?
- How will the ways in which humans acquire knowledge change in the future?
- Will human psychology be improved by gene-editing or medication?
- Will future human growth be free from environmental constraints?

Provoking Future Opportunities:

Business Insights

- Regardless of online or offline, more immersive learning experiences — such as platforms, equipment and contents — are needed to make learning more fun and inspiring across different contexts;
- Design different learning material and approach for different individuals that match their preferences and aptitudes, to better help people improve overall learning and thinking skills.

Marketing Insights

- Let brands assist education. Use brand professionalism in specific fields to teach students corresponding knowledge, so that brands can play a greater role in education;
- Learning is not confined by space. Accordingly, education platform and content have become strategically important focal points for brands. Actively look for opportunities for brands to collaborate with educational media, set up courses on relevant knowledge of brand-related fields, or sponsor similar lessons for brand promotion;
- We need to better utilize AI and machine learning technologies to more accurately identify individual preference and aptitude, in order to deliver more targeted courses to consumers.

3. Future Work

COVID-19 has hastened — and continues to accelerate — mass transitions of office work, relocating and reorienting it from traditional fixed workplaces to the more accessible realm of the digital. At the same time, many companies have started to experiment with alternative work models such as flexible work hours, work from home, etc.

With the expansion of reliable Internet coverage, supplemented by successive computer hardware and software updates, freelance opportunities have been inexorably on the rise.

Workplace has been witnessing rapid transformation as well, spearheaded by shared multipurpose workspaces such as WeWork®, whose ascendance caters increasing demand by entrepreneurs and freelancers alike. As a result, the traditional boundary between work and nonwork is becoming blurrier by the day.

Our questions: **In the future, how will the form and mode of work be transformed? What kind of work form is the best form to reach work-life balance?**

Prospect of Future Work

Digital Nomads: Work is My Frontier

Coco is an independent headhunter in AI/travel blogger. Being big on socializing and traveling, she's very happy about her current situation. Even when live streaming her travels all over the world, she always tried to meet as many local AI experts as she could, all to be quietly stashed away in her backup file.

Among the many challenges nomad life had brought Coco, a particularly taxing one that initially vexed her greatly was how to concentrate on the work at hand in everyday, non-professional environments. For this, she discovered VR office.

By the simple act of putting on a pair of glasses, VR office would relocate her visually to professional settings by displaying multiple voice-controlled or touch-activated windows, allowing her to edit documents, stream videos, replying emails, and other usual office activities. Better still, a holographic conference room could also be set up under modest conditions, enabling face-to-face communication with candidates and clients

regardless of her physical location.

Feeling a bit bored as of late, as was inevitable from time to time, Coco had been actively seeking new projects that piqued her interest. After some brief deliberation, she decided to join a global job sharing platform, which, on top of the usual job search site functions, sent her regular tasks for recruiting AI vetted candidates to projects that the site deemed they were suitable for. How to finalize the deal, naturally, is her call.

With each successful recruit, Coco also per habit, added another name onto her headhunting list, not to mention those perfect occasions to meet new people, which she now gleefully referred to as hitting three birds with one stone!

Keywords of future work trend

What we believe the future travel will look like:

Integration of Work and Life

Work Imitates Life vis-à-vis Life Imitates Work

Today, *work* is well on the way to be reconciled with a once antagonistic *life*. To be able to devote ourselves to works that we are deeply passionate about brings us much more happiness, as well as making us the writers of own stories.

Digital Nomads: work across space and time

Free choice of workspace, circumvent conventional spatial limits

On top of choosing work hours and locations more freely, we can also select from more flexible employment and teamwork models.

How does technology unlock this future?

With the rise of freelancing and π-shaped talents, digital, remote, and even virtual work — which bring a multitude of benefits such as reduced costs, expanded spatial limitation, increased multitasking efficiency, etc. — will likely become mainstream in the future. Predictably, major challenges such as how to facilitate real-time communication and interaction, or how to maintain individual professionalism outside of the office, will confront us as we move closer to a future of massive remote or virtual working. For now, it appears that we will have to be patient for related technologies as well as organization models to mature.

Aside from adapting to a different work sphere, we will also have to learn to efficiently coordinate our daily agenda — professional or otherwise — under an increasingly holistic approach to work and life, so we could reach the utmost of our potentials.

As such, digital nomads will be released from the rigidities of routinized daily lives and instead, have the time and space to be more creative, as much in life as in work.

The traditional wall between work and life will inevitably be torn down. By then, will you try to hold on to the familiar, or will you boldly accept new challenges this brings?

Optimistic anticipation and provocative critique about future work

Potential Benefits:

Easier Employment

Easier for disabled population and those with special needs to find work that are right for them

---

More Balanced, and Happier

The old antagonism between work and life is abolished, bringing about a general reconciliation

---

Freer

More options to choose from when it comes to work schedule and space, as well as employment models

---

Higher Efficiency

Artificial Intelligence and big data make division of labor more rational

---

More Intelligent Resource Allocation

Positions better matched with individual aptitude

More Control

Better life management and arrangement

More Accomplished

Easier to succeed when passionate

Meanwhile ...

Many existing jobs in the manufacturing and service sectors are forecasted to be replaced by AIs and robots, whose irreparable loss to humans will likely lead to the disappearance of traditional craftsmanship and perhaps more pressingly, unemployment. Will this fear of human replaceability exacerbate existing anxieties and lower the sense of security?

Furthermore, while automation significantly upgrades work efficiency, will its side effects — such as overcompartmentalized schedule, overstandardized work models, etc. — turn out to be less rewarding than anticipated.

Questions from Zhihu:

Will 5G give rise to any new professions?

What will be left to the humans after AIs replace most known work?

Will there be a groundbreaking technology that fundamentally alters — perhaps even comes to dominate — human beings in the future?

In the future where work-life boundary becomes unintelligibly blurred, how do we lead a good life?

Is UBI (Universal Basic Income) feasible?

Questions from Zhihu Expert:

Vincent Wang
Industry Insights Director, Baidu
Zhihu ID: Vincent Wang

I believe: Future hides in plain sight.

- Will there be a future where individuals no longer have to be "handpicked" by employers, and can instead search for the meaning of life?

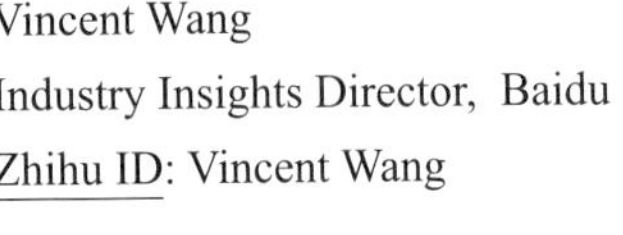

- What will future company look like? Will a robot be my boss?
- Will working in a cyberpunk world bring about more sense of belonging?

Xu Jun
China CEO, H+K Strategies,
Zhihu ID: XuJun

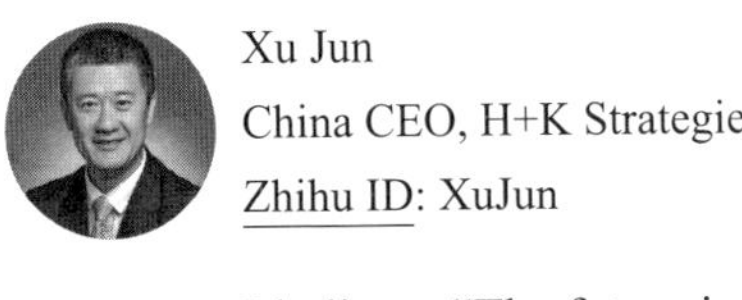

I believe: "The future is up" — that is to detect trend-setting information or signs of the foreseeable future, be inspired, seize the fleeting moments in daily routines and take a leap of faith.

- Works sustainable in the future are the ones that require inspiration. Are humans equipped with the genes for inspiration? Can they be repaired or reinforced?
- Should corporate culture encompass AI robots as they become critical components of the workforce? Should robots be compensated the same as human beings? Will Board of Directors include robot representatives?
- Will the man-machine, brain-computer or even brain-brain interface enable real-time performance evaluations and coaching, without interception of human emotions or unconscious bias or miscommunications, to ensure transparency and fairness?

Provoking Future Opportunities:

Business Insights

- Develop space and facilities with a more integrated approach to work and life, such as multipurpose workspace that have specifically designed furniture and appliances to accommodate consumer needs for more cost-effective work life;
- Provide third-party platforms for freelancers and digital nomads that share project opportunities; meanwhile, maintain existing T-shaped talent infrastructure to maximize respective effectiveness;
- Implement decentralized employment and work models, distribute workloads more rationally, efficiently, by AI and big data technologies.

Marketing Insights

- As the integration of work and life continues to fragment our ability to concentrate, new consumer needs will emerge to strategically address this change. Marketers need to capture and define new needs as well as their contexts to design relevant brand and product experience;
- The ongoing merger between work and life sphere will continue to redefine our daily lives, among which, work related media or platform will become important communication channels;
- Brands will participate in defining new lifestyles, while integrating brand ideals into the daily work-life, this will also bifurcate into something unique on its own.

4. Future Entertainment

At present, recreational experiences — be it online streaming or video gaming, window shopping or movie-going — still relies heavily on a fairly unbalanced distribution of specific technologies across space, such as internet connection, computer setup, public transportation availability, etc.

However, with the implementation of immersive techniques and technologies (3D/4D, holograms, AR/VR, interactive movies) gaining traction, the leisure sphere of the near future is likely to offer us much more fulfilling and easily accessible recreational experiences.

Our questions: **In the future, will entertainment still be like "entertainment"? And will we still be participants or take the lead in our own entertainment experience?**

Prospect of Future Entertainment (1)

Score Settled!

The Central Business District (CBD) bustled with people as lunch hour approached. Gooner and Kop, half occupying a crowded corner in a first-floor diner, was arguing about last night's Premier League derby.

"It had to be penalty, even I saw the foul there," Gooner was evidently unhappy about his team losing the match like that. "Hold on, let me show you," taking out his phone, Gooner found the 720-degree live-stream clip, and slow it to half speed. "See what I'm talking about? Isn't that guy pulling him from behind?"

"Well, football is ... you know, football, "Kop shrugged, obviously unconvinced.

"Careful there buddy, you doubting my judgment?" Gooner smirked, checked the time, and took out his VR glasses already. "How about we settle this on the field?"

"With pleasure!", taking out his glasses as well, Kop tapped his feet, clearly excited.

Having connected their glasses to the FIFA 2030 cloud server and their phones as joysticks, the two pals kicked off the game. With lunch hour virtual crowds started to gather in the audience, it was as if they were themselves there, competing first hand in last night's derby.

Prospect of Future Entertainment (2)

My Game, My Call

Ten-year-old Jack always thought of himself an archetypal American. Although for some reason, he had been extremely fond of Chinese Kong Fu as far as he could remember. Classic Kong Fu movie stars, from Bruce Lee, Jackie Chan, to Jet Li, Donnie Yen, he could recite their film performances backwards, if need be. Frequently practicing moves snatched from those movies, Jack dreamed of the day he could see himself actually sparring with them.

Fortunately, his techno-savvy dad knew just the way to make that dream come true.

As a birthday surprise, he took Jack to a media company by the name of *The Stuff that Dreams are Made of,* which provided customers opportunities to "act" together with AI stars that were reconstructed from an inexhaustible amount of complete film data.

Having completed a full holographic scan, Jack took the option to record his movement with a set of haptic equipment — a few blows in thin air here, a dozen hops there would allow the AI to further deconstruct

his natural state, and create more accurate, credible simulations.

All was set.

Under a midnight full moon, on top of the Forbidden City, Jack met a "Jet Li" in full wuxia armor. After traditional greetings, each took his pose — the game was on. For three whole minutes, phantom Jack dodged and parried as though fish in water, and a silent Jet Li receiving and defusing his relentless advances, real as life.

"That was so ... oooo cool!", exclaimed dad as they drove home, the complete clip already transferred to their family cloud and Jack, in his wild excitement, had naturally posted it on all his social media accounts.

"Ikr? I couldn't wait to see my friends tomorrow — Jack the Kong Fu star! Ha! This is much more fun than selfies with celebrities. You remember Marc? Last month, he went all the way to ...."

As Jack droned on, dad slowly tuned out. In his mind, he saw Audrey Hepner, tall and tan and young and lovely, gently taking his arm, promenading by the ocean, together to their New York Holiday.

Keywords for future entertainment trend

To Immerse or Not to Immerse

Connect anytime anywhere to immersive experiences

With the rapid development and inevitable popularization of 5G — or even 6G — technologies, sketchy internet connection will become a thing of the past, replaced by reliable internet anytime and anywhere. At the same time, we hope that more authentic recreational experiences will be supplemented by exploring deeper into currently unchartered territories such as those enabled by immersive VR/AR technologies.

Emotional Immersion

Participate and lead, unfold your own story

We no longer have to remain mere spectators to music, film, games, or other narrative-centered entertainment. Instead, with the help of interactive designs, we could actively participate, or even lead as protagonists, in story-making, which revolutionizes the way we relate ourselves to traditional ways of recreation.

How does technology unlock this future?

5G network will bring us constant reliable and high-quality connectivity; meanwhile, cloud technologies (e.g., storage computing) will enable us to circumvent barriers imposed by traditional data storage and have uninterrupted access to our choices of entertainment anytime/where.

At the same time, supplemented by groundbreaking technologies such as AI and AR/VR, motion capture and 3D simulation, etc., recreational experience will become substantially more immersive.

Finally, we will be many steps closer to mastering our own leisure sphere, by choosing contents that are more relevant to us, even actively participating in unfolding the narratives ourselves (choosing different plots or endings as protagonists, etc.).

How do you want to dominate your entertainment experience in the future?

Optimistic anticipation and provocative critique about future entertainment

Potential Benefits:

More Immersive

More sensually authentic

More Customized

Personalized contents and perspectives

More Connected

Connect gaming devices anytime/where

More Fun

More creative storytelling

More Interactive and Creative

Active participate in the unfolding of narratives

Smoother connection

Goodbye to unstable connection

Leisurizing Life

Entertainment anytime/where

Meanwhile ...

Will the barrier-free taken-for-grantedness of future recreation inundate our senses and push us into ever more atomized — or even extreme — pursuit of entertainment?

Moreover, will over-leisurizing life make existing addictive disorders more pronounced?

Questions from Zhihu:

Will the Metrix become reality one day?

Will virtual celebrities replace offline ones in the future?

Hypothetically, if humans were to mass immigrant to the Minecraft world, what would the world be like in a thousand years?

If two certified, highly competitive future-forecasters were to play rock paper scissors, who would win?

When virtuality becomes real, how can we better navigate the two worlds?

Questions from Zhihu Expert:

Eric Wang
Creator Growth, Tencent
Zhihu ID: tiao-deng-kan-jian-65

I believe: In the future, technology can replace physical manpower, but it cannot replace emotional interaction.

- Will future entertainment take place more in the real world or the virtual world? Can people in the future choose to immerse themselves in the virtual world forever?
- In the future, will the pleasure of entertainment exceed the boundary of human's cognition?
- What is the "final" form of content transmission?
- Will content creation in the future be done by fewer creators or majority?

Ken Wang
Brand & Marketing Consultant, Ex-Marketing GM of Xingmei Group
Zhihu ID: kk-wang-27-26

I believe: In the future, you can enjoy the whole universe without leaving home!

- If there were a time machine, would Doraemon be born earlier?
- How to define the boundaries between legal constraints and law enforcements that may be involved in future

entertainment, and how to prevent breaking moral rules?

- Will the future entertainment be more dominated by virtual games or imagination, and then create a real environment and scene?
- Will entertainment be redefined? Can people maximize happiness from the best balance of individuals and groups' activities?

Provoking Future Opportunities:

Business Insights

- With the onset of 5G and potentially 6G technologies, faster and more stable recreational services should be provided;
- Provide more unimpeded interconnectivity support, allowing players to connect with friends on different platforms anytime anywhere, and enter different game worlds;
- Provide multi-sensory (visual, auditory, smell, touch, etc.) immersive entertainment experiences (such as games, sports events and concerts);
- Allow consumers to get more involved; let consumers participate in the design of products and contents and create an experience together.

Marketing Insights

- Push brands to participate in the process of building everyday leisure, whether it is product design, ad contents, online and offline interaction so that brands can have a more

important role in consumer leisure life;

- More immersive entertainment marketing will spawn more storytelling and interactive communication methods and contents;
- Explore and identify different consumer entertainment needs and scenarios to accurately design and build in-depth brand experiences with the help of more immersive platforms, devices and contents.

5. Future Consumption

Traditional retail has begun to transition into smart and experiential retail, albeit at the moment, there is much room to grow due to technological constraints and the like. As a result, today's so-called sensations such as *new retail* and *digital experience store* do not have substantial difference when compared with traditional retail, not to mention that the overall shopping experience remains pretty much the same.

That said, a hopeful glimpse into something fundamentally different is on the horizon, especially in e-commerce. Take for example, Taobao's product feature *QianrenQianmian* (*A Thousand People, A Thousand Faces),* which is among the most high-profile use of big data and machine learning to provide individual consumers with highly specific advertisements and products — is a promising start indeed.

Our question: **In the future, how can we balance rationality and emotion to make consumption decision that generates the highest value?**

Prospect of Future Consumption

Le coup de foudre

Inside a vintage perfume store, a thriller was set in motion.

A single gunshot shrieked out, tearing apart the tranquil veneer of a moonless night.

Unhurried, echoes of the shot meandered through empty nocturnal alleys of fin-du-siècle Paris, rippling past sentry-like street lamps that, embalmed in the midnight mist, shone particularly pale against the cobblestone road, still were wet from the earlier rain.

A silent silhouette darted across the street, behind it pursued a few gesticulating cops. They were herding the fugitive shadow into a dead end.

Succeeded at last, they surrounded the shallow alley, somewhat hesitant to step across the line between wavering light and immutable darkness. The cops blinked wearily at each other, as if arguing who should go first. All of a sudden, to everyone's surprise, from the lightless corner a few feet away, catwalked out a young

woman. In an impeccable black evening dress and a pair of velvet gloves of the same color, her lips were scorching rouge, eyes emerald, as though possessed by a feline spirit. Hanging carelessly from her marble-like neck, was a necklace of stunning beauty. On it was the priceless diamond that was just now reported missing from the museum.

With a modest smile, the nameless woman waltzed past the ranks of uniformed men — all of whom had by now transfixed into living statues, and disappeared into another street corner. Lingering in the air was the only trace left of her — that mesmerizing scent of a flowering jimsonweed, irresistibly elegant, lethally sweet.

Frame by frame, the mysterious alley under frowning clouds, the lamp-postified cops waking up from an unspeakable dream — all of it faded out. Lights came on. It was the familiar interior of the perfume store once again. In the air, however, dawdled the intoxicating scent, refusing to disperse.

The show, as it turned out, was part of the store's latest offline flash mob program, aimed at promoting better immersive shopping experience with customized content. And apparently, it hit home again. Among an ocean of eager customers, one young woman wriggled her way to the counter and asked, still with evident excitement, "Excuse me, but what was that perfume?"

"This is our *Moonless*, "answered a smiling young man, "the particularly memorable scents — which

you just experienced — are its middle and base notes. Inebriating, isn't it?"

Without hesitation, she made the purchase. To her delight, she noticed that the package was imprinted with a rouge lip print, just like the nameless woman would have left by a dreamy kiss. Replaying the elegant waltz in her head, the girl ambled out of the store, a big smile hanging from cheek to cheek.

Keywords of future consumption trend

A Thousand Hamlets in a Thousand People's Eyes

Personalized or customized shopping experience

Identity recognition technology and big data analysis bring more personalized shopping experience, which more accurately caters individual consumer's mainstream or at times, highly particular preferences and demands in areas such as store design, merchandising, and hospitality.

Such 360-degree customized experiences are considerably more efficient vis-à-vis conventional consumption via, among other things, actively promotes sustainable prosumption by reducing waste produced from mismatch.

In all likelihoods, there will be more similar approaches that more fully utilize maturing data technologies to guide consumers in making individually meaningful decisions.

Shoplaying

Experiential retail, diversifying choices

Traditional offline retail will be diversified via the implementation of emerging technologies discussed so far, providing more novel and pluralistic consumption experiences such as story-themed, party-themed, exhibition-themed shopping, etc.,to stimulate and fulfill consumer curiosity. In the meantime, retail venues can also provide on-site entertainment, simultaneously serving as a place to influence and guide consumers in discovering trends that pique their varying interests.

How does technology unlock this future?

In the foreseeable future, consumer *pursuit* for personalized products as well as services will evolve into a *need* for tailor-made shopping experiences. Among offline retailers, big data will be widely utilized in providing highly customized services. Such stores are likely to be thoroughly compartmentalized based on specific preferences among key demographics, complemented by customized sensory and interactive designs, in order to lead individual consumers to an indelible impression that this is my place.

Meanwhile, offline shopping will become more multipurpose. Integrated experiences of entertainment, aesthetics, fashion and shopping, such as the holographic experiences generated by spherical panoramic virtual display technology (during which product placement can familiarize the consumer with the product on more intimate grounds), will make shopping substantially more fun and ultimately, a new way of life.

To which brand are you a loyal consumer? If you were the CMO of this brand, what kind of shopping experience would you envisage for your customers?

Optimistic anticipation and provocative critique about future consumption

Potential Benefits:

More Experiential

Diverse shopping experience integrating entertainment and practicality

---

More Efficient Supply Chain

Upgraded efficiency within the production-consumption cycle

More Inspirational

Guide consumers to pursue better lives through diverse scenarios and contents

---

Easier to Choose

More relevant information to help with decision-making

More Customized

Highly customized product interface, merchandising and services

☹ *Meanwhile ...*

Will consumption choices that are habitually reliant on algorithm suggestions push us into the consumption equivalent of *Information Cocoons*, irreversibly narrowing down our horizon?

Will transition into experiential consumption marginalize rational decision-making, and prompt more impulse consumption?

With trends of further digitization, will certain physical products — and perhaps more importantly, the idiosyncratic temporal and spatial significance they embody — gradually recede out of materiality altogether?

Questions from Zhihu:

Is there a place in the future for physical stores?

How sustainable are e-commerce models that rely on live streams? How will it adapt to the future?

How will sustainable products influence future consumerism?

Questions from Zhihu Expert:

Jing Wang
Founder and Chief Knowledge Officer, SOCIAL ONE
Zhihu ID: DizzyWhale

I believe: True generosity to the future is to give the present everything.

- At a time when data-based technologies help brands to learn more about consumers, while helping consumers to learn more about themselves, will future consumption become more rational or more emotionally oriented?

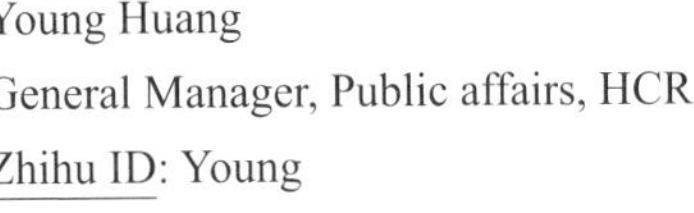

Young Huang
General Manager, Public affairs, HCR
Zhihu ID: Young

I believe: Buckle up with change, hold yourself tight.

- Will the forbidden box be opened in the future? For example, will you implant brain chips to improve your children's IQ? Will you choose to re-write your child's genes because of worrying about disease?
- Online consumption has nearly revolutionized its offline counterpart, what might in turn post similar existential challenges to online consumption in the future?

Provoking Future Opportunities:

Business Insights

- Based on historical data, anticipate consumer needs and more proactively provide highly customized products or services. Meet consumer needs for personalization through product design, selection, and customer service both online and offline;
- Increase overall supply chain efficiency by arranging production and resource allocation based on consumer needs;
- Create more imaginative, contextualized utilization of products to inspire pursuits for higher quality of life.

Marketing Insights

- Insert more diverse experiential zones at key points in major shopping routes (such as holographic product demonstration, etc.) to influence consumer decision-making vis-à-vis particular brand, thereby increasing marketing efficiency;
- More accurately identify scenarios for potential demand with more targeted, contextualized information to inspire and condense consumer decision-making path;
- Design more imaginative, experiential retail models, promote cross-industry cooperation, and promote more multidimensional retail function and experience;
- Brands are pioneers in inventing novel consumption models. As such, they should clearly identify their distinct advantages and experiment with different kinds of contextualized experiences.

6. Future Home

Over the past few decades, boundaries of more and more homes have faced constant incursion by demands from work and leisure, concerns over publicity and privacy, etc. The trend has only been aggravated by the ongoing pandemic. That said, this uneasy transition also gave rise to more versatile home devices, such as cleaning bots and voice-control appliances. At the same time, devices that track and monitor elderly and children for safety purposes, both when indoors and outdoors, are being accepted by more and more families.

Our question: **What will home be defined as in the future?**

Prospect of Future Home

Tenderly, into that Good Night

At 8:30 in the evening, the VR firework show I had been planning for the past month — from researching to designing each feature, down to the last detail — lighted up the small patch of artificial sky in our fifth-floor apartment.

Twenty years ago, under a clear night sky, Marie — with whom I had hopelessly fallen in love a year before — and I were married.

As the summer sun sunk deeper into the immense shadow of the Earth, we lay motionless in bed, trying to relive the sweet and sour memories each and every blossom overhead brought to mind.

"Twenty years ...." Fireworks continued to rap around us, but she seemed to have not noticed them at all. Breathing, inhaling, again, and again. Soundless, like a phantom.

"Hmm ...." Marie grunted softly in my arms, as if already halfway asleep, ready to leave all this splendor for some distant sweet dreams.

Closing my eyes, I pressed her hard against myself, wanting to breathe in all of her, to hold on to this most tender, ephemeral scent, to lock her soft flesh in my delirious embrace, to never let her go.

"Miss me?" broken, garbled sounds finally escaped, racing at her, caressing her visage with a world of lost words, an ocean of swallowed tears.

A nod, then another.

Starting to turn around, the tender body in my arms disintegrated, pixel by pixel — trickled, like yesterday's sun, into toady's shadow.

Five years ago, on our fifteenth anniversary, back from a firework show under a moonless sky, fate took her, to dreams that she would never tell me about.

Keywords of future home trend

Home+

A multipurpose home

Along with the gradual integration of work and leisure, the future home will be a multipurpose place for work, entertainment, learning, socializing, parenting, etc.

Smart Family Members

Smart butler

The ongoing advancement in smart home and IoT technologies will make future home life more intelligent and convenient, by implementing tools that can more accurately identify and meet the needs-both material and emotional — of residents. All family members — even pets — could receive real-time health management and care.

How does technology unlock this future?

Being surrounded by smart home devices and wearables undoubtedly makes everyday life much easier, and more efficient. If being able to independently complete rudimentary tasks represent the first step in smart device evolution, we are likely to witness rapid, substantive progress in the coming decades that will make the already smart devices truly intelligent. Under the advancement of IoT and machine learning technologies, future home devices will not only be able to learn by themselves and adapt to the specificities of different homes, perhaps they would even become sentient in some capacities, providing much personalized services to each resident. Unsurprisingly, this will gradually change the outlook of smart homes from relying on independent, single-purpose devices to multipurpose connectivity powered by inter-device "group intelligence".

At the moment, AI and holographic technologies are still independent from each other. However, ongoing trends suggest that the integration of the two are rather inevitable. Coupled with high-speed internet, we will be able to communicate — just as we do with each other — with holographic stewards that are in nearly every regard, perfectly human.

Senior Digital Experience Designer/Lin Juying

In my opinion, the development of intelligence comes in three stages:

natural, autonomous, and adaptive. *Natural* means that interactions within specifically defined contexts are more human like, rather than rigidly mechanical; *autonomous* signals the capability to actively extend operational limits through self-learning; finally, adaptation builds on the previous two, which gives the entity the flexibility to accurately and spontaneously adjust itself to unencountered situations.

When technology offers highly accurate surrogate companions that know us in most intimate ways, will we still be looking for human companies?

Optimistic anticipation and provocative critique about future home

Potential Benefits:

More Comfort

Capable of identifying needs and solutions for different family member, both material and emotional.

More Personalized Lifestyles

Offer suggestions for your lifestyle, from clothing to diet, work schedules to entertainment plans.

More Security

Facial recognition access control system, high-definition, real-time monitoring connected with mobile devices

---

More Free Time

More thoroughly liberated from housework

More Options

A multipurpose place for work, entertainment, learning, socializing and parenting

---

More Novelty

Changing home theme at a finger snap

More Organized

Smart systems will also contribute to general management

More Caring

Real-time care for elderly people, kids, even pets

Meanwhile ...

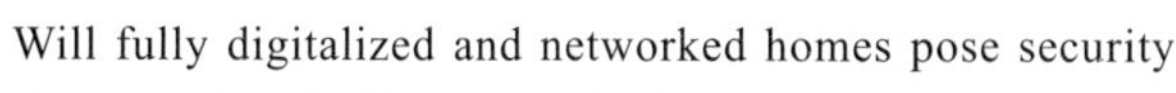

Will fully digitalized and networked homes pose security threats against family assets and privacy?

With those who can afford rapidly upgrading high-tech products and services having access to better homes, will it transition into yet another front in an array of already widening class inequalities?

Questions from Zhihu:

What is your ideal family life?

How will future homes be designed and developed?

How will traditional Chinese family structure change in the coming decades?

With the continuous integration of work and life, what is your ideal future home?

How can we make family life better in the future?

Questions from Zhihu Expert:

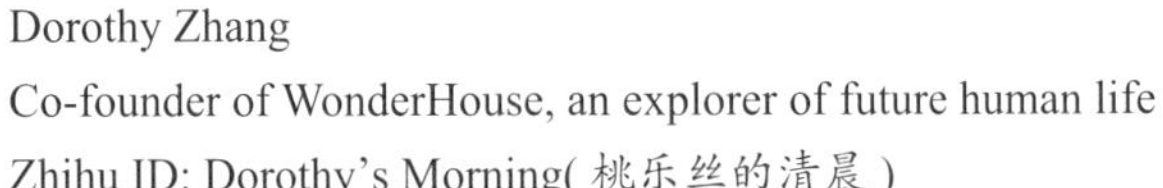

Dorothy Zhang
Co-founder of WonderHouse, an explorer of future human life
Zhihu ID: Dorothy’s Morning(桃乐丝的清晨)

I believe: To master is to progress, to expand, to awe and to reflect.

- In addition to parents + children, how else would future families be structured?
- What kind of home and communal environment would you like to spend your old age in?
- How can one be with their loved ones after passing away?
- How will future family bonds be sustained?
- Will human bodies regress in the face of the deluge of smart home devices?

Louise Lv
Head of China Digital Hub,Philips (China) investment Co., Ltd.
Zhihu ID: Lisa (丽莎)

I believe: In the future, life will be more convenient, communication will be easier, social division of labor will be more segmented and professional, but at the same time, the social network may be more circle-based and niche.

- Will family members communicate more closely or more alienated in the future? How will the relationship between family members be affected due to the "information-island effect" and the possibly widening generation gap?
- In the future, can the experience/knowledge of elders be transferred to the next generation through chip/data?
- Will intelligence permeate every life scenario in the future? For example, the smart refrigerator can visualize everything in a menu including storage days, recipes, order and deliver home with one click.
- Due to the development of data and technology, will people get used to enjoy a comfortable life rather than try to make change?

Sabrina Li
Chief Designer, Lead8
Zhihu ID: Badmood (林不爽)

I believe: Tomorrow will be better.

- Does the future family need to be defined by marriage still?
- What kind of attention and care will young children and the elderly receive in future family life?
- Will future income be allocated on a household basis rather than on an individual level?
- How can resources such as food, clothing, housing, and transportation be better balanced in the future and shorten the gap between the rich and the poor?

Provoking Future Opportunities:

Business Insights

- Design smarter home products or systems that can identify material and emotional needs of family members to provide accurate, contextualized solutions, in addition to flexible space utilizations for comfortable home life;
- Improving home life efficiency in areas such as increasing device effectiveness, thus further automating traditionally manual housework, giving residents more free time;
- Develop more advanced security and monitoring apparatus, whereas in the digital realm, perfect cybersecurity software to protect home networks and personal data from counter

potential cybercrimes.

Market Insights

- Clearly define the advantages and disadvantages of different scenarios and solutions to help brands more smoothly become part of family life; at the same time, promote cooperation between different brands and design comprehensive marketing strategies;
- Devise personalized communication content and solutions — such as dietary, work, leisure advice — for each family member;
- More accurately identify device users and corresponding contexts, such as family get-togethers, to more accurately match contextualized contents with particular family members.

7. Future Community

Currently, most Chinese communities are still designed with the singular aim of residential housing accommodation, whereas more socio-ecologically sustainable communities are far from becoming mainstream.

One example of what a future community would look like is Wujiaochang in Shanghai: an integrated neighborhood with easy access to basic social amenities from education, grocery, healthcare to work and recreation.

Our question: **Will the future community help realize what life should be like?**

Prospect of Future Community

Virtual Mah-jong, Real Friends: A Glimpse into an Eco-social Community

Zhang, in his early 70s, was initially against moving to the newly completed eco-social community. "You young people just don't understand what neighbors mean!" was his go-to protest whenever the topic was brought up.

As an old schooler, Zhang could hardly imagine a life out of the kind of traditional residential communities that he grew up in, and never once thought of leaving over his long and taxing years. For Zhang, to greet familiar faces on his way back from morning jogs, to play a few rounds of mah-jong or chess in the afternoon with his old comrades meant nearly everything. When he first heard of those newly developed communities on the far side of town, boosting their fairy tale like convenience (one-stop service station everywhere — Ha! Imagine that! Whoever needs neighbors anymore?), an indignant wave of arm and a loud grunt were his only response.

But after two years of relentless campaign by the daughter, Zhang took out the white flag and waved it with shrugged shoulders. On the moving day, knowing his irreversible defeat, some more murmurs of "young folks just don't know anything about community anymore" could be heard trickling from the back seat of the car.

After settling Zhang in, his daughter and the husband left in mid afternoon, having half a day's work to catch up to. Having watched the door closing itself behind the leaving couple, Zhang sat down by the family dinner table that was passed down from his great-grandfather. Reading glasses perching precariously on the tip of his nose, he squinted at that blank, beige wall on the far side of the living room, for the moment seemed to be lost in thought.

"I would've been finishing that chess game with ....", halfway through, the doorbell unexpectedly rang, interrupting the fresh mumble.

Outside stood two smiling young women. *Hmm, they look kind,* Zhang thought. Nonetheless, he realized himself still eyeing them somewhat suspiciously, a few paces away.

"You must be Mr. Zhang, our new resident", the right one started softly, evidently trying to break the ice, "I'm Jane, this is Jules, we are from the community center. Would you mind if we come in and show you around a bit? The place might seem empty, but it's full of smart

home devices that might seem a little strange to you at first”.

“Sure, come on in, give me a tour then”, stepping aside to let them pass, he smiled a bit awkwardly, remembering that for a moment, he thought they were going to sell him those useless junks that he had seen at his daughter’s place.

Sitting down at the table, Jules took out of a pair of glasses that looked not much different from the one that’s still on Zhang’s nose

“This is our community developed smart glasses, would you like to try it on?” Zhang took off his own, and put the pair. “The glasses will take a second or two to adjust to your eye conditions, so please don’t panic if you see blurs everywhere,” as Jules was saying, his vision — that was from a blurry blob for a second — came into focus again, and much clearer than before. “Is it better now?”

“Yeah. Yeah. Boy this is quite something,” Zhang heard himself saying, trying to remember what was the last time he saw things this clearly.

“Wonderful. Now, aside from customized vision, it’s also connected to the internet, as well as everything else in your home — it’s responsive to voice command,” Jane was saying. “For example, if you want a specific newspaper, just speak the name, and it can read you the news”.

Slightly dizzy from the newly acquired 20/20, Zhang tried to look around. Previously empty space was suddenly full of stickers, on each was detailed instructions on their utility and succinct instruction manuals. "You can also have them read out to you if you don't want to read yourself, like the newspaper." Seeing him nodding slightly, Jules continued. "We have one-stop service station on the ground floor in each building, you could go down and pick whatever you want — in case you don't feel like walking out, just order some in the glasses, and we'll have them delivered right up. There is a community hospital right next to this building as well, if you feel the need, just let us know," Jane tapped her glasses softly, "we'll have a GP or expert coming up as soon as possible".

Just as she finished, Zhang's glasses sent him a loud notification, almost startling the old man. "This is probably from your friends who moved over before you, they're trying to connect with you just now. If you'd like to accept their friend requests, just nod at the notification would do".

Nodding as instructed, Zhang saw — to his complete surprise — that it was his friend Li, who moved out from the old neighborhood some months ago.

"Li! How ... how did you? I don't remember seeing you walk in!"

"Who said I'm here, eh?" grinning, Li explained that this is virtual call, much better than those sketchy video

calls on a computer screen. “If you don’t want to go out,” Li continued, “let me call Fang and Sun next time, we’ll have a few rounds virtual mah-jong, as good as face-to-face, just like old times!”

The women left in another half hour, having shown him a bit more of his new home. Walking them out of the door, he slid the glasses down his nose and looked back at the deceptive emptiness, then slowly pushed them back up with a smile.

Perhaps it’s not that bad, after all.

Keywords of Future Community Trend

What we believe the future travel will look like:

Ecologizing Community

More multifunctional and socio-ecologically sustainable

Community Centers

Socio-ecologicalizing:

- More multipurpose and easier access to necessities such as healthcare, daycare, work, education, shopping, socializing, etc.
- More healthy life management system

De-fencing:

- Individual residential compounds no longer administered as separate units but instead, integrated into broader communities that have fuller access to basic social

amenities.

How does technology unlock this future?

At the moment, community development by and large stops at optimizing or upgrading existing function. By contrast, future communities will reinvent community life — thereby the entire urban landscape, by merging currently unconnected communities into new residential blocks that in addition to providing easy, reliable access to basic social amenities, also use more sustainable management strategy to ensure the integrity of the local ecosystem.

The ongoing trend of digitalization will inevitably lead to future communities with built-in high-tech connectivity, enabled by big data, 5G, IoT, smart wearables, etc. As such, they will evolve past traditional models of top-down community planning and in its place, institute more horizontal management (volunteering, civic duty rotation among members, etc.) that takes into account the needs and wants of every community member.

Furthermore, such horizontal approaches will make communities more self-sustaining as socio-ecological units, increase community resilience, thus effectively alleviating city administrative pressure.

Will future multipurpose communities with ubiquitous, automated one-stop services make us more socially independent from each other?

Optimistic anticipation and provocative critique about future community

Potential Benefits:

More Liveable

More sustainable relationship between residents and local ecosystem

---

More Convenient

More multipurpose with comprehensive social amenities such as healthcare, daycare, work, education, recreation, etc.

More Resilient

Horizontal community management allows more timely and effective intervention in public emergencies

---

Resource Sharing

Resource sharing with different communities for communal improvement

---

More Social

Richer in cultural and social activities, brought by cultural and creative industrial parks, etc.

More Connected

More boundary-less communities to facilitate broader exchanges

Meanwhile ...

Will potentially uneven socio-ecological development of communities lead to unequal resource distribution (such as unfair access to educational and healthcare facilities)?

Will largely automated and concentrated social amenities coupled with reliable easy access to internet services diminish the incentive to socialize, and lead to individuals becoming more insulated from each other?

Questions from Zhihu:

In the next decade, what changes will technological advancement bring to our communal lives?

Will co-living become mainstream?

What public spaces do you wish to have in your future community?

Will the current lack of neighborhood bond and communal culture change in the near future?

Questions from Zhihu Expert:

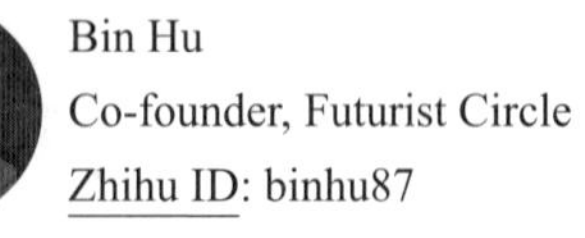

Bin Hu
Co-founder, Futurist Circle
Zhihu ID: binhu87

I believe: Futures, unpredictable, only creatable.

- Will the psychological bond between people become looser or stronger?
- Will matriarchal societies be reestablished?
- Will blood ties disappear in the future?
- Will there be a future society that is entirely sustained by shared hobby or interest?
- How would we reinvent human social structures on Mars?

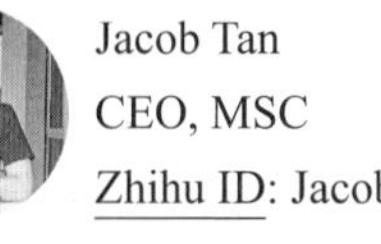

Jacob Tan
CEO, MSC
Zhihu ID: Jacob

I believe: Technology for the rich, genetic mutation for the poor?

- Will happiness become incrementally more difficult to obtain?
- Will the melting glaciers and compressing habitable space bring new conflicts?
- Which will come to direct future consumption, trust (emotional ties) or fact (hard data)?

- How far are we from explicitly sanctioning digital slavery?
- How will equal rights and diversity discourses evolve?

Provoking Future Opportunities:

Business Insights

- Inter and intra-community ties will help transition communal space into unique socio-ecosystems. It is paramount that future businesses learn to adjust to potential needs from this transition;
- Industries must achieve greater synergy and cooperate with government resources in creating multifunctional communal landscape. At the same time, internal community functions should be brought up to date — technologically and socially — to provide more convenience one-stop amenities;
- Generate unique communities based on local and regional specificities which on top of attracting more relevant commercial entities, simultaneously sustains healthier socio-economic local development.

Marketing Insights

- Based on the socio-ecological connectivity that underpins future communities, platforms and media through which such connectivity is maintained will inevitably diversify, making the community a crucial space in which businesses interact with consumers, while trying, at the same time, to bring about qualitative breakthroughs in communal marketing;

- Due to the more finely compartmentalized nature of internal future community functions, brands need to provide more relevant and effective communication platforms to accurately anticipate and cater consumer needs to become an integral part of the communal space;
- As such, more space will be opened up for brands to introduce their own cultures and ideas into different communities, which can bring in more novel elements to facilitate healthier community development.

8. Future Health

COVID-19 has turned public eyes once again to the healthcare industry, while pushing it beyond its traditional industrial boundaries, deepening exchange with other sectors. Meanwhile, *Healthy China 2030* campaign was launched under the auspice of full policy support, with the aim to promote affordable, accessible and accountable public health services.

Our question: **In the future, can we more easily manage the health of ourselves and our families at different stages of life?**

Prospect of Future Health

Who said they were just AIs?

Sunday afternoon, an indoor badminton court.

Carole hunched slightly, clenched the racket, knitted her otherwise soft brows, eyes alert on the young man who was posing to serve. A seemingly careless tilt of the wrist sent the ball whooshing across to the net, but it was too high! She stepped back and pounced on it instantly, noticing this oversight, sending the ball back with a mirthless smash. The young man grinned. Instead of being caught off guard, as she was sure would happen, he darted to the net, and with a textbook hairpin net shot, dropped the ball in her forecourt, as effortlessly as before.

Too far to catch the ball, Carole shook her head at the scoreboard, slightly vexed, and picked up the ball, ready to serve again.

A few rounds later, the game was over. Opposite to a panting and sweating Carole, the perfectly composed young man suggested to call it for a day, to which

she nodded in agreement. In the blink of an eye, the stadium, the court, the sparring partner all faded out, and around her was a bright empty room.

It had become a weekend routine for some time now, this VR simulation badminton lesson with the personal health manager by the name Xiaowind — an AI that had been with her for nearly a decade now. Chatting with Xiaowind on her performance just now by way a weekly summary, who was just saying, "Compared with records over the past month, you've apparently improved quite a lot ...." Listening quietly to updated numbers from return rate, reflex interval to heart rate, calorie burn, and body fat percentage — which decreased a further 3% over the period — Carole strolled homeward in the warm afternoon sun.

But the last item caught her attention. The already relaxed browed knitted themselves together again. "Say, Xiaowind, isn't this a bit too slow? Is there anything I can do to accelerate it a bit?" Sensing her slight agitation, the soft, even male voice replied, "No worries Carole, you're doing fine, try to enjoy the moment".

"Really? Nothing," still she sounded unconvinced.

"Of course. You know what I noticed lately? You've been way too anxious on my diet and fitness plans for you — which, might I add, you carried out to perfection! Relax. Chill. Lay back for a minute. Naturally, I want you to be fit and healthy, but don't forget to smile and pat yourself on the back once in a while, will ya?"

Releasing a long sigh, Carole's brows unknitted themselves one last time on that sunny afternoon as she reached her third-floor apartment. Putting on soft jazz, a mild smile hung modestly on her cheeks, refusing to disperse, all the way through the rest of the day.

Keywords of future health trend

What we believe the future Travel will look like:

Smart Health Management

A comprehensively designed healthcare industry covering all life stages

- The concept of comprehensive health runs through the entire life cycle with different prevention, control and intervention at different stages;
- Pluralistic conception of health: body, mind, appearance, lifestyle, family, social relations;
- Comprehensive system with personalized plans, providing accurate services;

More systematic personal healthcare system from monitoring, prevention to diagnosis and recovery.

How does technology unlock this future?

"Prevention first, treatment second" will become the primary model for future healthcare, with health management, precise testing, treatment, and recovery ensuring overall public health. At the same time, with Medicare for all supplemented by commercial medical insurance, medical expenditures will

continue to decrease for the public.

Furthermore, high-tech devices, such as wearables, remote treatment and chronic disease monitoring, and healthcare blockchain, coupled with AI, IoT+, and other cutting edge technologies will revolutionize medicine to such an extent that precise personalized professional healthcare management will no longer be mere dreams.

Founder and CEO of Xingshulin/ZHANG Yusheng:

In the next three decades, we will face a rapidly aging society. With more than half of the population about to enter the over-60 demographic, it is crucial that the healthcare industry starts to address the countless foreseeable dilemmas that will be brought by this inevitability now.

What possibilities does a healthier self open you to?

Optimistic anticipation and provocative critique about future health

Potential Benefits:

Healthier All Around

Improve mental in addition to physical health, along with healthier lifestyles

---

More Attentive

More organizations to provide healthcare services

More Efficient Healthcare

Remote diagnosis and treatment technologies that more effectively allocate resources

---

Easier Disease Prevention and Control

Real-time, fast and accurate monitoring of health metrics

More Precise Solutions

Efficient diagnosis, analysis, precise judgment, leading to the best solution

---

More Equitable Resource Allocation

More targeted healthcare, shared digital medical records and universal Medicare system will greatly improve potential conflicts generated by unequal resource allocation between higher and lower tier cities

---

More Assurance

More control over personal health to better plan for the future

Meanwhile ...

While digitizing healthcare system is indisputably optimizing personal and collective health management, it is yet to provide solutions to pressing dilemmas such as obesity from lack of physical exercise, eyesight deterioration from screen overuse, loneliness from social marginalization, etc. What new

challenges will healthcare transformation bring us? And how can we better respond to new disease outbreaks?

Health tracking and monitoring technologies give us access to possess real-time health situations of our own bodies, but will this encourage overreacting to bodily changes that we do not fully understand (especially among children and elderlies) and cause hypochondriac tendencies?

Development in anti-aging medicine will further blur clearly identifiable distinctions in physical appearance between ages, will this change drastically alter the ways in which we interact with each other?

Questions from Zhihu:

What diseases could be eliminated in the foreseeable future?

Can future medicine completely eradicate myopia?

Has Forward Head Posture (FHP) already become a trademark of modern humans? In what ways can it be prevented?

How will public healthcare evolve against the backdrop of global ageing?

Questions from Zhihu Expert:

Ann Lim
Chief Client Officer, Wavemaker China
Zhihu ID: Hedonistann

I believe: We underestimate the impact of now on the future — the challenges we face today become the natural force to find solutions for the future. In our continuous quest to be better, a state of superhuman will emerge in the future.

- Can mental stress be eradicated?
- Can physical fatigue be totally prevented?
- Will more than 80% of healthcare be delivered virtually?
- Do surgeries still need to be operated by (human) doctors?
- Can we modify our physical body appearance independent of surgery, diet and exercise?

Echo Chen
Brand Doctor, LeSweet (sugar-free sugar brand)
Zhihu ID: A worm in door (门里一条虫)

I believe: Freedom, equal rights, individuality.

- When long life expectancy becomes standard, what else do we want?
- Will truly effective and harmless weight-loss medication be invented?

- Will there be passive fitness schemes that can maintain health without physical exercises?
- Will there be more types of sports that break our physical limits in the future?
- Will big families that share the same space among multiple generations still be desirable?

Provoking Future Opportunities:

Business Insights

- The healthcare industry has become a focal point in recent years: with the continual upgrade in living standards, people have correspondingly increased their demand for better healthcare. As such, businesses can capitalize on this trend and take the industry into account while diversifying their own organization;
- Comprehensive monitoring: develop context-specific healthcare devices such as for home, office, public space etc. One way to achieve this is to integrate them into home and/or office furniture, public facilities, and so on, to track and monitor in real-time the health of oneself, family members or employees, so that emergencies can be met with quick and accurate solutions.

Marketing Insights

- All industries can try to connect and introduce healthcare into their own marketing, for pharmaceutical and other

medical enterprises no long hold a monopoly on it;

- Completely integrate brands into day-to-day life to promote healthy lifestyles — both on the individual and societal level;
- Marketing agencies and platforms can try to promote industry integration, helping brands across industries to devise more comprehensive service models for consumers to achieve healthier lives;
- Discover different healthcare needs across specific contexts to accurately match marketing contents to suitable solutions, such as associating different health products with fitness schemes.

9. Future Social Life

With the expansion of traditional leisure and work sphere, individual social networks are gradually pushing beyond their conventional boundaries. Among other things, social media platforms play a critical — and increasingly foundational — role in extending, as well as maintaining existing online + offline social circles, not to mention keeping the multitude of identities we have to switch between diverging contexts in sync with our different selves.

Our question: **In the future, how will more complex social relationships and multiple identities broaden the width of our lives?**

Prospect of Future Social Life

Alone Together: Traversing between Dimensions

Sam always thought of him a hopeless nostalgic one. If given a choice to between now and some bygone times, he would, without hesitation, leave the technological matrix of now for a simpler, more human-centered past.

Yet despite still being overwhelmed on a daily basis, Sam did by chance discovered some technologies that eventually made him feel more at home. Instead of diving into the heart of metropolitan restlessness and be anonymized into just another face scanned among weekend crowds, Sam for most of the time preferred to instead, turn off the alarm clock, sleep in a bit, make a nice brunch, read a little in a very comfy couch, and put on his black glasses.

In an instant, Sam the luddite — as his friends long ago playfully nicknamed him — was put in hibernation, and in his place, Sam the classic was summoned up.

A founding member of the Nostalgia Society, Sam

had the luck to charter a whole planet, fondly named *Nostalgia* — as HQ, in the global network of digital universe where the society was based. Here, on this Earth-sized virtual planet, free from spring sandstorm and winter smog, unknown to rancid landfill and floating plastic continent, Sam welcomed all kinds of visitors — humans and AIs — to this meticulously manicured, spotlessly timeless dream world of his. If it were a nice day, he'd pop on his early 20th century clothing, hop in one of his classic ford convertibles, pick up Coco — his virtual girlfriend who "lived" a few blocks away from his favorite house — and spend a whole weekend that he once jokingly called, to Coco's amusement, *our little cheek-to-cheek.*

Some days, they'd alight at a random vinyl store, pick a record blindfolded, and listen quietly under the dim, orange light for the entire afternoon; or to the local flea market, if they felt like it, where Sam was particularly fond of a leather goods vendor — every time they met, they'd talk for hours about the by now nearly extinct traditional shoe or handbag craftsmanship, and the unique, rich history behind it.

As his planet attracted more visitors, the society's membership boomed as well, and many wished that they could meet each other face-to-face, offline, at some point.

Over the past month, plans to offline events were finalized and this weekend, Nostalgia Society rented venues in many cities to host nostalgia theme parties

that would, Sam hoped, boost society popularity, while at last let online friends meet each other, without separated by a screen. At the end of the two-day event, more people walked into the venue that Sam was overseeing than he had imagined, many of whom, after brief VR trials of life on *Nostalgia,* eagerly signed up society membership, all the while providing a plethora of feedback that Sam thought would tremendously benefit the incoming upgrade of the planet.

In time, Sam became a nostalgia celebrity, quite contrary to his initial reluctance towards fame — to whichever degree. Among other things, his latest fashion creation that fused nostalgic designs and craftsmanship with contemporary techno-minimalism became as popular as that solitary, crowded, but homely digital planet of his.

Keywords of future socid life trend

What we believe the future Travel will look like:

Multiple Selves in Parallel Worlds

Different identities for different space

With rapidly diversifying professional demands, hobbies will become a main driver in enlarging existing social circles. One such example is the *slash* movement (Alboher, 2012), which, on top of fusing together traditional work and leisure sphere via extensive technologically sustained personal networks, it also transforms the meaning of the social and makes individual

lives increasingly pluralistic.

As such, we can take further steps to imagine that perhaps even our social identities or nationalities can be virtualized, further opening our lives to endless possibilities.

How does technology unlock this future?

As the fragmentation of our daily lives continue at an unprecedented rate, the need for novel, sustainable, and pluralistic ways to maintain, on top of expressing different selves has never been more pressing. As a result, experimental parallel worlds such as Facebook's Horizon — a VR social platform — is a welcoming attempt to address this challenge.

In the next 5 to 7 years, we are likely to see the rise of massive online digital parallel worlds, which will qualitatively eclipse their predecessors — i.e., digital social worlds in online forums and MMORPGs (Massive Multiplayer Online Role-playing Games) — in bringing more meaningful second lives. Furthermore, virtual identities may even be integrated into the offline identification systems and open up undiscovered frontiers for conceiving *who* we are.

Insight and Education Innovation Expert/Candy Yang

In the future, instead of the online subjected to the offline, the reverse will happen, such as bringing new friendships and job opportunities. Maybe we can arrange a personalized life more effectively with the help of online life, i.e., spending more time on things of personal interest and value.

Among the seemingly inexhaustible identities virtual worlds promise to offer, which ones do you crave the most, and what kind of lives do you wish to lead under them?

Optimistic anticipation and provocative critique about future social life

Potential Benefits:

Broader Horizon

Cultural barriers between regions are easier to overcome

Career Growth

Expanded social circles offer significantly more social capital networking, thereby bringing more career opportunities

---

Richer Life

Virtualized identities (potentially nationalities), enabling otherwise un-intersecting lives to be experienced from different perspectives

---

Low Maintenance Upkeep

More media through which ties with different social groups can be maintained

---

Better Social Skills

More occasions to socialize, leading to better social skills

Easier Access to a Sense of Belonging

Easier to find like-minded people and communities

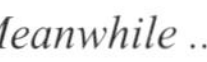

Meanwhile ...

Will long-term immersion in virtuality — communicating with others or not — misguide some to unreal expectations for offline reality, leading to psychological issues?

The polarization of opinions on social media is becoming an important issue, against which we have yet to find effective solutions. Will it spiral out of control to the extent that the *spiral of silence* is normalized as an unavoidable part of daily life?

With social circles becoming more specific — even professional — in design, membership threshold is becoming higher as well. Will future social network maintenance demand disproportional amount of effort in sustaining different semi-professional identities, which, instead of bringing joy and relaxation, become anxiety-inducing and harmful to our wellbeing?

Questions from Zhihu:

What will future social network look like? Are current socialization models sustainable?

Can social phobia, or social anxiety disorder, be alleviated in virtuality?

What virtual identities do you want in the future?

If you are given the choice to have virtual nationalities, what kind of virtual country do you dream of joining?

Questions from Zhihu Expert:

Sean Liang
PR Director, Soul App
Zhihu ID: Soul App

I believe: However will future technology be developed, people should be an end rather than mere means.

- Will humans still have the need to meet new friends?
- Will the offline reality still be where most people socialize?
- Are AIs friendable?
- Will telepathy be realized by technology?
- Is human consciousness digitizable?

Lao Bo
Adquan, CEO, focusing on brands, communication industry, integration of strategy and creative with an aim of building a super bridge
Zhihu ID: Laobo (劳博)

I believe: Communication facilitates human progress.

- The Internet has met enormous needs for online

communication, yet, with prolonged exposure, will the desire to communicate offline gradually dissipate?

- Which is the most convenient way to socialize, face-to-face meetings, or anytime anywhere online communication?
- Should professional online communications retain their conventional formality or be casualized as everyday chats?
- What are the most difficult issues to communicate? Is human communication progressing or regressing?

Provoking Future Opportunities:

Business Insights

- When developing platforms or products, social features need to be prioritized to provide consumers with more social benefits;
- Develop convenient high-tech tools to help people from different regions and cultural backgrounds communicate with each other, such as speech recognition and translation tools;
- More segmented and vertical social tools and platforms to help more people to find like-minded friends and communities.

Marketing Insights

- Brands should be more involved in the creation of social topics to guide and promote the establishment and dissemination of mainstream social values;

- In the future, more platforms will “transform” into social platforms to provide brands with more in-depth communication opportunities. This requires a clear understanding of the roles and values of different emerging social platforms, and a more detailed social marketing matrix design;
- Find more segmented and precise social platforms and communities for brands to communicate with target audiences more accurately, especially for consumers with multiple identities, it is necessary to identify different needs in different communities and scenarios to improve the effectiveness of communication.

10. Future Data Asset

With the digital realm becoming an increasingly indispensable part of our lives, public awareness on the whereabouts of the staggering quantities of data that we create on a daily basis has accordingly become a major concern. Yet, legislators have been slow to legally recognize personal data as individual property, which makes it nearly impossible to know — let alone control — to where or to whom our private data flows once it leaves our devices. As a result, data leak, thief or illegal use are still not uncommon.

Our question: **Will our data become an asset or a burden of redundancy?**

Prospect of Future Data

Doubled, Just Like That?

When Henry checked his long-neglected data bank account, he couldn't help but to gawk at what was in front of his eyes. It turned out that the value of his consumer data rights — without obtaining which, third parties could not by any means acquire access to these information — had nearly doubled during this latest episode of involuntary forgetfulness.

Coming to think it, Henry realized that he was probably overreacting a bit. After all, over the past year, the newly engaged man had been fairly preoccupied by the enormity of wedding preparations — from searching economic package deals for home appliances and furniture to planning the actual event, he spent hours after hours perusing online comments, comparing utilities, even haggling from time to time — as a proper perfectionist would. At last, when all items on the to-do list were finalized, Henry acquired a complete data log from the e-commerce platforms as usual, tossed the file to his data bank under the label *wedding preparations* to not be confused with dozens of other files that were already there, and nearly forgot all about it — until just

now.

In his absence, the bank had already assigned his long-term personal AI assistant to sort out the data, filing each item — furniture cost-effectiveness, best wedding venues in the regions, etc. — under related headings, posted it on the market for open bidding, as Henry had requested. Not surprisingly, having invested that much, his package remained quite popular despite the radio silence to leasing or purchase inquiries.

Among the bidders were the usual suspects — hotels, airline companies, travel agencies, and what have you. Although this time, he noticed a good number of daycare centers, pre-school education institutes, and even a few real estate developers, all appeared to be perfectly eager in planning a future for him.

"Hmm, didn't figure I'd be this popular", drumming his fingers on the table, Henry grinned, failing to suppress a tingling feeling that he were in fact a minor celebrity of some kind. Halfway through the grin, a notification popped up, unexpectedly announcing that a new bidder had just raised another 10% for his health data — a series of files that had been under continuous compilation, and unrelated to the wedding ones. Intrigued, he opened the report again.

It was a sports recovery center. The institute happened to be experimenting a medication against sudden heart failure from over-exertion, to which, Henry being a fitness enthusiast, his health bracelet data would

contribute a good deal.

Having done some brief research on the center, and still buoyant on the gleefulness from earlier, he decided to share all the health data files with the institute without charge, for it was Henry's firm belief that more than its commercial value, personal data should also contribute to a collectively better future.

Henry was in ecstasy all afternoon.

Keywords of future data trend

What we believe the future travel will look like:

Data Becoming Asset

Personal data become asset with legally protected ownership

Under the advancement of digital technologies, personal data will become personal asset. As such, it can be deposited in data banks and can only be used by third parties upon owner authorization — which, on top of making personal data more secure, also calls for novel ways in which digital assets can be efficiently utilized.

How does technology unlock this future?

With more clearly defined ownership structure around personal data, it is but a matter of time that it evolves into a currency or a goods that can be traded or sold like others. The urgency, therefore, of sound data management is going to be great. We think that data banks based on blockchain technologies will

play a vital role in safeguarding future security of our digital portfolio.

Meanwhile, increasing demands in data security will give rise to new professions as well as business opportunities, such as data security consultancy, data insurance, data-free resorts, etc. All of which will perfect ways in which — under strict legal premises that recognize and protect private data ownership rights — personal data can be more efficiently shared and utilized.

5G Expert/RUI Bin

5G is exponentially faster than existing communication networks. As it generates a significantly larger amount of information, at the same time, it also brings greater challenges to data security. Inevitably, data will become personal asset in the future and will be shared via more sophisticated encryption.

Among all your personal data, which ones do you think are most priceless?

Optimistic anticipation and provocative critique about future data

Potential Benefits:

Safer

Data security will undergo upgrade when it becomes personal asset

More Privacy

Depositable to data bank, private data can only be accessed with owner authorization

---

More Valuable

Personal data can be cashed or traded as private asset

More Customized

Analysis and usage can be carried out with proper authorization, which generate more customized products and services

---

More Control

Future data ownership will exclude tech giants — who currently control most of our data — from the ownership structure, and grant the individual complete legal rights over the data they generate.

Better Planning

AI aided reviews and analyses of personal data to make better plans

Meanwhile ...

Will the explosion of information volume brought by newer generations of communication technology compound existing dilemma concerning the digital realm, and irreversibly complicate our daily lives to such an extent that it might lead to certain insurmountable obstacles on data manageability at some point?

Will the legalization of private data ownership give existing cybercrimes such as pirating, tampering or fraud, more fertile and maneuverable grounds?

Questions from Zhihu:

In the era of big data, what intriguing transformations will we witness in our daily lives?

In the future, how do we escape a potential matrix?

How can data help us better review the past, or inspire the future?

How will current business models that reply on targeted advertisement based on taken-for-granted personal data access evolve in the future?

Will immortality without corporeal appendage become reality if all information stored in the brain could be converted into uploadable data?

Questions from Zhihu Expert:

Jason Zhang
Director, Xiaomi Inc.
Zhihu ID: digication

I believe: Human beings may evolve into new species with reaching the whole universe.

- Can future memory data be collected on a chip and put into

the brain?

- If everything is digital in the future, is this world still real?
- If the future connection no longer relies on the Internet, what will it rely on?
- What happens if you can get the data of anyone's life at will?

Lisa Guo
Managing Director of Programmatic and Platform Services, GroupM China
Zhihu ID: Lisa

I believe: Any future is unpredictable. Undoubtedly, technological development will make life, work and communication more convenient. No matter which future technology ushers us into, the trust, compassion, and mutual responsibility that underpin human societies will endure. That said, we still need to consciously make our digital future a human one.

- In the future, will data ownership — separated into public vs private data — be given clear legal recognition?
- Will data become an asset that can be bequeathed or inherited?
- Will the sheer quantity of future data generate a mostly unmanageable excess of information under which we are buried?
- Will highly specific professions such as data trash cleaner emerge in the future?

Zhang Honglei
Book Editor, Huxiu.com
Zhihu ID: Lonely Book Club(孤独图书会)

I believe: The future for humankind will get better and better — that is, until the singularity is reached.

- Is there a future for ordinary people in a world dominated by big data and algorithms?
- How to protect our privacy in the era of big data?

Provoking Future Opportunities:

Business Insights

- Data banks are likely to become mainstream once individual ownership is legalized;
- Data exchange is also likely to be established, with more data transaction models and data products;
- Provide customized services based on different data dimensions.

Marketing Insights

- As a result of data privatization, new ways of managing this asset such as open-sourced data centers are likely to give rise to different exchange models for digital information;
- More efficient ways to generate value out of raw personal data need to be devised, in order to promote the roles future data plays in marketing;

- In-depth analytical cooperation is needed among different service providers to better understand consumer data, match and design more customized brands, products, and services;
- Brands should lead in responsibly managing and utilizing personal data, for instance, Apple IOS14 requires user authorization to access other devices in the same network, by way of restricting third party accessing user personal information.

Epilogue

Our journey into the future is at last, coming an end.

In a time when change is everywhere in the air and innovation the everyday buzzword, we find ourselves constantly at crossroads, prepared or otherwise, treading into the future and try as we must, to claim it ours.

The tales of this book is our attempt to illuminate that journey. We hope that by now, with your curiosity fully awakened, you have in mind some preliminary sketches about that uncharted temporal frontier — and with some effort, many more questions accompanying.

In a positively better future when guided progress of science and technology, culture and economics have further freed us from quotidian routines to fulfill our varying potentials on both the individual and societal level, we will be — more so than ever before — the writers, directors, and actors of our own stories. All that is needed is the boldness to challenge what is in front of us today, and the audacity to imagine radically different tomorrows.

We believe that to participate in shaping the future is no longer to dream a pretty daydream in our time, thanks to ongoing trends of technology democratization and customization. Instead, the increasing level of symbiosis between technological enablers and their human creators foretell a time in the not-so-distant future when each of us can choose or design for themselves the lives they wish to lead, be it a clean restart from past dissatisfactions, or a continuation of proud traditions.

We hope when looking back from the future, you will give an affirmative nod to the choices you made today, and find the thoughts pulsing through your mind right now worthwhile.

We welcome and encourage you to search "Questions on the Future" or "Questioning the Future" on Zhihu, and join us in *Our Question to the Future* discussion board to share your unique questions with others.